BUYING A PERS

RAID - Redundant Array of inexpensive DISCs
(Splitting data between multi Than
one Hard disc)

BUYING A
PERSONAL COMPUTER

How to choose the right equipment
to suit your needs

Allen Brown

2nd edition

How To Books

Author's dedication
To Teresa for all her smiles

Acknowledgement
The author wishes to thank Mike Geary and Martin Ansell for carefully
reading through the draft copy and making many helpful suggestions.

Cartoons by Mike Flanagan

British Library Cataloguing in Publication Data
A catalogue record for this book is available from the British Library.

© Copyright 1998 by Allen Brown.

Published in 1998 by How To Books Ltd, 3 Newtec Place, Magdalen Road,
Oxford OX4 1RE United Kingdom.
Tel: (01865) 793806. Fax: (01865) 248780.

First published in 1996.
Second edition 1998.

Note: The material contained in this book is set out in good faith for
general guidance and no liability can be accepted for loss or expense
incurred as a result of relying in particular circumstances on statements
made in the book. Technical and legal matters are complex and liable to
change, and readers should check the current position with the relevant
authorities before making personal arrangements.

Produced for How To Books by Deer Park Productions.
Typeset by PDQ Typesetting, Stoke-on-Trent, Staffs.
Printed and bound by Cromwell Press, Trowbridge, Wiltshire.

Contents

List of Illustrations

Preface
to the Second Edition

This book is intended for the reader who is thinking about buying a new PC and wants to make sure they are buying the most appropriate model for their needs. It deals exclusively with the PC and not the Apple Macintosh or any of its variants. The world of the PC is shrouded in a bewildering cloud of technology and this may appear quite intimidating to the inexperienced new user. This book will explain what the technology is all about and how it affects your choice of a PC model.

It's quite possible that the capital outlay for a new PC will represent a substantial amount of money. You will therefore want to make sure that you don't end up with a white elephant or find out at a later date that you failed to consider something which is going to incur extra costs. Much of the information in this book will help you to avoid making costly mistakes when choosing and specifying a new PC system.

This book will:

- Introduce you to the technology that goes into today's PCs.

- Help you to make the right choices when buying a new PC for a specific need.

- Help you to select the most appropriate peripherals to add to your PC (such as printers and fax units).

- Help you to consider the range of software products available for your needs.

- Introduce you to what's needed to access the Internet (the Information Superhighway).

- Make you aware of the many exciting possibilities and applications for your PC.

9

- Enable you to make informed judgements if you decide to upgrade your PC in the future.

As you read through the chapters you will come across examples where commercial products have been cited. These are mentioned to provide examples of what's available in the market and should not be regarded as recommendations for the products.

Definitions

In this book there are many terms and expressions that are frequently used in the world of the PC – no profession is free of its jargon. Where such jargon is encountered an explanation is provided as to its meaning and significance. Further explanations can be found in the glossary at the end of the book. There are, however, a few fundamental definitions that need to be introduced before you begin:

- **Bit**: information is held in computers in a digital format that has two states, 0 or 1 – these are called bits. All information, whether text, sound, images or any other format, can be represented by having combinations of 0s and 1s. The transfer rate of information is measured in **bits per second** (bps) and this is an important measurement for performance. In general the units will be:

  kbps (1,000 bits per second)
  Mbps (1,000,000 bits per second).

- **Byte**: when eight bits are collected together they form a byte and it is commonplace to measure memory capacity in terms of bytes. You will often come across:

  kbyte (kilo byte – 1,000 bytes)
  Mbyte (Mega byte – 1,000,000 bytes)
  Gbyte (Giga byte – 1,000,000,000 bytes).

- **Bus**: digital circuits usually have multiple parallel channels along which bits of information flow and these are referred to as buses. Common bus widths are 8-bit, 16-bit, 32-bit and 64-bit. Normally the wider the bus the greater the information flow rate.

- **Data**: this is a term often used when describing information held in a digital format in computer memory. For example, you may have the text of a book held in computer memory – this is an example of stored digital data.

- **Frequency**: in the digital world the frequency of events is measured in **Hertz** or **Hz** – number of events per second. In particular **clock frequency** is often used as a measure of a PC's speed. You will also come across:

  kHz (kilo Hertz – 1,000 Hertz)
  MHz (Mega Hertz – 1,000,000 Hertz).

- **Microsoft Windows**: when buying a new PC it is highly likely that you will have Windows supplied with it as standard. This is an **operating environment** in which software programs will run. More details on this product are given in Chapter 4.

After reading this book you will realise why the PC offers so many possibilities in almost all walks of life and why it has become the most versatile tool of the last quarter of the twentieth century. You will also appreciate why a good working knowledge of its operation should form an important part in the training of a professional whatever their chosen field.

PC technology has been rapidly changing since the introduction of the PC in the early 1980s. The second edition of this book is a response to the changes that have occurred over the last year and how they have affected the range of products on the market.

Dr Allen Brown
Cambridge 1998

Is This You?

Housewife

Landlord

Accountant

Social worker

Computer programmer

Schoolteacher

Author

Designer

Industrialist

Undergraduate

Architect

School pupil

Lecturer

Club owner

Manager

Retired

Electrical engineer

Post-graduate

Production engineer

Self-employed

Doctor

Secretary

Policeman

Researcher

Publisher

Veterinary surgeon

Computer engineer

Solicitor

Maintenance engineer

Club secretary

Musician

Military officer

Lawyer

Photographer

Civil engineer

Businessman

Estate agent

Entertainer

Salesman

Mechanical engineer

Agent

Stockbroker

Writer

Manufacturer

Engineer

Librarian

Laboratory worker

Shopkeeper

Archaeologist

Probation officer

Chemical engineer

Book-keeper

Electronics engineer

Farmer

1
Selecting a PC

The world of the personal computer (PC) is as exciting as it can be bewildering. Over the past five years in particular, PC technology has progressed to quite extraordinary levels. There is certainly plenty of technology but what's missing are the people to use it efficiently. When a new technology is introduced into the workplace the missing component is the appropriate level of skill training. In many instances the new user is expected to acquire new skills using their own initiative. This is certainly true if you are buying one for the home. Buying a new PC and getting it right requires a certain amount of knowledge. It's so very easy to fail to take into account the cost implications of your needs and you may find yourself paying far more for the PC than you originally budgeted for.

UNDERSTANDING THE PC TODAY

In the majority of offices and schools and now in many homes the PC has become a standard piece of equipment. Its general purpose design allows it to be customised to a large variety of applications. This means that a PC can be configured to perform several functions for its owner. It is therefore important that an appropriate configuration is defined to fulfil the needs of its user. By this we are not talking about a particular model but about the PC's features and add-on features (**peripherals**). Today's PC can be interfaced to a vast range of peripherals ranging from image scanners to laser printers and from bar-code readers to electronic musical instruments. It is therefore useful not to think of a PC just as a stand-alone piece of equipment but more as a component in a larger system. Fortunately PCs are very flexible and can be modified to accommodate new needs as they arise.

Networking
In many companies and organisations, the PCs are **networked**

Table 1. What are your PC requirements?

Requirement	High	Medium	Low	Unknown
		Weighting		
Wordprocessing	☐	☐	☐	☐
Spreadsheets	☐	☐	☐	☐
Databases	☐	☐	☐	☐
Games	☐	☐	☐	☐
Good quality printing	☐	☐	☐	☐
Colour printing	☐	☐	☐	☐
Accountancy software	☐	☐	☐	☐
Presentation software	☐	☐	☐	☐
Diary (weekly and daily)	☐	☐	☐	☐
Desktop publishing	☐	☐	☐	☐
Fax facility	☐	☐	☐	☐
Storing lots of data	☐	☐	☐	☐
Networking PCs	☐	☐	☐	☐
Drawing software	☐	☐	☐	☐
Drafting software	☐	☐	☐	☐
Processing pictures	☐	☐	☐	☐
Information Superhighway (the Internet)	☐	☐	☐	☐
Picture image-scanning	☐	☐	☐	☐
Music systems with keyboard	☐	☐	☐	☐
Multimedia	☐	☐	☐	☐
High quality graphics	☐	☐	☐	☐
Good quality video	☐	☐	☐	☐
Playing audio CDs	☐	☐	☐	☐
Producing CD-ROMS	☐	☐	☐	☐
Archiving material	☐	☐	☐	☐
Mathematical modelling	☐	☐	☐	☐
Training	☐	☐	☐	☐
Programming	☐	☐	☐	☐
Developing software	☐	☐	☐	☐
Making patterns	☐	☐	☐	☐
Writing articles and books	☐	☐	☐	☐
Learning new IT skills	☐	☐	☐	☐
Book-keeping	☐	☐	☐	☐
Bilingual wordprocessing	☐	☐	☐	☐
Language translation	☐	☐	☐	☐
Producing pamphlets	☐	☐	☐	☐
Speech recognition	☐	☐	☐	☐
Making a PC video	☐	☐	☐	☐
Digital photographs	☐	☐	☐	☐
Making audio recordings	☐	☐	☐	☐
Computer aided design	☐	☐	☐	☐
Producing multimedia materials	☐	☐	☐	☐
Cookery reference	☐	☐	☐	☐
Making labels	☐	☐	☐	☐
Home and garden design	☐	☐	☐	☐
Music composition	☐	☐	☐	☐
Artistic drawing	☐	☐	☐	☐
Writings essays for school, college or university	☐	☐	☐	☐
Research for postgraduate qualification	☐	☐	☐	☐
Radio ham applications	☐	☐	☐	☐
Writing technical reports	☐	☐	☐	☐

together to form a computer **Local Area Network** (LAN) that allows the PC users to access common facilities. These facilities may consist of hardware features such as printers or software packages such as wordprocessors. On a computer network, only one copy of a particular software package will exist, but all the users will be able to access it as required. Networking may not appear to be an issue, but even if two PCs are operating in the same room it's worthwhile thinking about the network option. This is covered in greater detail in Chapter 7.

Networking with a modem
The PC can also gain access to other networks using a **modem** via a telephone link (see Chapter 5). For example, you could be anywhere in the country and link up your computer to your company's main computer system. It's likely that you may also require access to **on-line** services using your PC. Generally referred to as the **Internet** or **Information Superhighway,** its significance as an information source has grown enormously over the past few years. This is covered in greater detail in Chapter 6.

WHAT DO I NEED FROM A PC?

It's quite possible that you already have, at this stage, a pretty good idea of why you want a PC. In addition you may even have some other future needs lined_ up. Whatever your needs, you want to ensure that you get the best PC system for your money. To help you plan for your present and future requirements, use Table 1 which is a list of PC applications. Each entry has alongside it a range of boxes for you to enter a weighting appropriate to your situation.

Thinking about your needs
Table 1 will help you to think about not only your current needs but also possible future requirements. At this stage you might not know what you want from your PC in the future. However, after looking through the table you will at least be aware of the possibilities. The idea of the list is to see everything that you need to consider and to attach a level of significance to each entry. It will also serve as a prompt for applications of your PC that you had not previously considered. As you work through the body of this book it will become clear how most of the entries in the table can be realised by means of a PC and whether they are likely to be of interest to you or other users of the PC.

HOW MUCH SHOULD I PAY?

Having defined your needs you will find yourself in the unenviable position of setting a budget or maximum spend for a computer system. The emphasis is on computer system and not computer because a computer alone will do nothing for you, you will need software and peripherals. Your costing must therefore include the PC, the software (don't rely on illegal copies from your friends) and the peripherals to support the PC. If you intend to use a complicated software package you may even have to include training costs as well in your budget.

Points to consider before buying
- Don't spend all your budget on a top of the range PC before estimating your other needs. Otherwise you may learn the hard way that you can't afford the software or the printer you need.

- Remember to include the cost of the software – don't think that you can get a copy from someone else. The software licensing agreement only allows the software to run on one PC at any one time. It is illegal to have the software running on more than one PC at any one time unless you have a network licence for it.

- A useful rule is that of 'even quality'. Don't pay out for an expensive PC and couple it up to a bargain basement matrix printer – you will soon recognise the mismatch and regret it. If you buy a mid-price range PC then match it with mid-price peripherals.

Budgeting for a PC is not easy for the simple reason that you are unlikely to know what you really need at the outset. On the other hand, buying an inadequate model will leave you frustrated and you will incur additional expense trying to upgrade it.

Shareware
Some software packages are free and these are often referred to as **shareware**. Much of it has been written by hobbyists and may have poor levels of protection. Some of it is good, but it is worth remembering a quote from the American economist Milton Friedman: 'There's no such thing as a free lunch'. This is just as applicable to software as to other aspects of life. Shareware can cause problems for your PC – there are no assurances with it. I write from bitter

experience having lost the entire contents of a hard disc because of a poorly written shareware package. The lesson is to treat such packages with caution.

Prices

Towards the end of this chapter you will find a number of case studies of typical PC configurations and their approximate prices. There are roughly three bands of PC prices, namely:

- Low end   £400 – £1,000
- Mid range £1,000 – £2,000
- Top end   £2,000 – £3,000.

Although these are the price ranges for the PCs alone it is highly likely that you also require a printer. Before you plan your budget make sure that you read the section in Chapter 5 on computer peripherals.

You may come across PCs cheaper than £400 based on older designs. You must be cautious of these as they may not run software written for today's PCs. However, it's quite possible that your application does not need a current model. If this is the case it might be worth while considering new, end-of-season hardware. One well-known supplier is **Morgan Computer Co.** Tel: (0121) 456 5565.

BUYING A PC FOR THE HOME

The number of PCs sold into the home market increases year by year and for many people the versatility of the PC justifies the expense. There is a whole range of domestic applications where the PC can be of value. Just looking at Table 1 will remind you of the possibilities. One of the prime motivations is the extensive number of games that are available for the PC. Many thousands of working hours have gone into the creation of some quite spectacular PC games. Coupled with high quality graphics, superlative sounds and other multimedia features, they have become an essential part of life for many a growing teenager.

Buying a multimedia PC

When buying for home use you should ensure that the PC is equipped with the facilities to run multimedia software (Chapter 3 covers all aspects of multimedia). A multimedia PC will require a CD-ROM drive (now standard in most new PCs), a microphone and a sound card. Multimedia PCs also come with loudspeakers, although the quality of the speakers is often suspect. If you are paying out a lot of money for a PC it may be worth while buying a separate, small-scale hi-fi unit (with a CD player) which will serve the PC much better than multimedia speakers. You will often find that sound cards come with a microphone and leads to link the card to the hi-fi unit. The supplied microphone is usually mono and not of particularly good quality.

Using the PC for home education
The educational value of the PC is frequently stressed and it is important if you are buying a PC for this purpose that you know exactly what you want from it. For example, one of the major failings within the secondary education system in Britain today is the poor level of mathematics attained by the majority of pupils. Software packages such as Microsoft's GCSE Maths (CD-ROM version) can be very useful in complementing maths learning.

However, they are not complete solutions as they still require actual tuition. This will be true for almost all subjects, not just maths. As far as secondary education is concerned the PC can only complement what already exists.

Doing the family accounts
If you wish to use the PC for book-keeping purposes then you will not be disappointed. There are several software packages on the market designed for just that. **Microsoft Money**, for example, is a low-cost financial package for monitoring investments, income and expenditure. It can also be used to estimate the cost of loans.

THINKING OF YOUR PC AS AN INVESTMENT

If you are buying a PC for pleasure or as a luxury item then you soon find that it's got at least one thing in common with a new car: it's going to lose you money owing to its alarming high depreciation rate. This is a fact of life. What was a top of the range PC two years ago costing over £2,000 is probably now worth less than £400. You will find that when buying a new PC today its specifications will exceed a two-year-old model originally costing twice as much.

Investing in a PC
If, however, you are buying a PC as an investment then your frame of reference will be quite different. You will probably be buying the

PC for a business venture, and a return on investment will therefore be crucial. A number of scenarios are possible, for example:

- The PC system is bought to facilitate your current business operations and to assist or replace time-consuming clerical functions.

- The PC system is bought specifically for a single job or contract and its cost forms part of the tender. Once the job is over the investment in the PC will have been recouped and it can be used for the next job.

- You are setting up a facility where a PC system will play a key role and the customer base is not yet fully defined. The PC system should be bought only after a careful review of the market for your service or product. Only buy what you need – be critical. You will need to recover its costs within an acceptable period – usually less than nine months.

- You may be thinking of buying several PCs and want them networked together. This is covered in greater detail in Chapter 7.

Recovering the costs

When buying a PC as part of a business operation you need to justify its costs and recover your capital outlay as soon as possible. Its justification should be included in your business plan only if it is an essential item. If it's not essential don't buy it because it will be under-used. You can ask yourself one very simple question:

- If I buy a PC for business how much time will I or someone else be using it?

To justify its expense, the answer to this question should be several hours per week. Anything less and it will be a wasting and depreciating resource. For example, if a PC is bought for a secretary, it ought to be in use the whole time that she is working which could be 40 or more hours per week. Efficient use of a PC is normally very time-consuming and you'll only really need it if you're likely to save time by using it to replace existing tasks or if you introduce new essential tasks. It's not a good idea to buy a PC on the off-chance that you will use it occasionally or in the future.

BUYING SAFELY

A question that often arises is where is the best place to buy a PC. Your main choices will be either a mail order company or a high street shop. The all-important rule is, never pay cash or by cheque, always pay by credit card. If something goes wrong with the PC and the supplier goes into liquidation while it is still under warranty there is a reasonable chance of recovering your repair costs from the credit card company. Normally they will have a reimbursement insurance policy scheme to cover these problems. If you've paid cash there's a greatly reduced chance of getting your money back. Even famous names in computer supplies go under. Remember it's a highly competitive market and most of them operate on wafer-thin profit margins.

Protection schemes
Sometimes there are other fall-back schemes. For example, if you order a product advertised in the magazine *PC Direct* and something goes wrong, they operate a **Mail Order Protection Scheme** (MOPS) to help you recover your money. In general you would be extremely unlucky if you were not able to recover some of your money.

Being aware of hidden costs
One way that mail order companies try to increase their profit margin is through the hidden extra of delivery charges. It is not unknown for some companies to charge £10 for delivering a single CD-ROM which could have been posted for 50p in a jiffy bag. Look out for delivery charges – it may not be necessary for you to have next-day delivery which carries an extra premium. PCs normally require a burn-in period as they are constructed as and when ordered. Two or three days is the normal burn-in period. Why pay for next-day delivery when you have to wait at least four days?

Buying from high street shops
High street shops, although very accessible, do not always offer the best deals on the products they sell. With a mail order company, you can specify exactly what you want, not what happens to be on the shelf at the time as you'd get with a high street shop. However, with a high street shop you don't have to pay delivery charges.

Rules to remember

Wherever you choose to buy your PC from, there are a number of simple rules that you should observe:

- Always use your credit card to make payments for PC equipment.

- When dealing with mail order companies, get written quotations (three is normally regarded as a minimum). Unfortunately quotations are not legally binding but they normally have a period of validity (30 days usually).

- Always confirm your order with a written document. If there are disputes with the company this will act as the decisive testament to your order.

- Look out for hidden charges such as next-day delivery and insurance.

- If you are uncertain about any aspect of the purchase try and get the opinion of someone who knows about PCs to clarify the uncertainties.

- Don't forget about VAT, currently at 17.5 per cent. Most PC advertisements do not include VAT in their prices. VAT is also charged on delivery costs.

All new PCs come with a warranty and an after sales service, but not all warranties are the same. Again there could possibly be hidden costs.

Looking at warranties

Having bought your new PC you would like to feel secure in the knowledge that if something goes wrong then you can have your PC repaired free of charge and if all else fails replaced with a new one. A warranty on a PC system will normally last for one year from the day you purchase it – this is a provision of the **Sale of Goods Act**. There are still questions that you should consider. How do you determine the length of time it will take for the manufacturer to effect a repair and what charges are you likely to incur?

When you buy a PC there could be as many as three parties involved:

- The supplier that you bought the system from.
- The manufacturer of the system.
- The company holding the service agreement (the warranty). Sometimes the supplier will hold the service agreement as well.

When something goes wrong
If something goes wrong and you contact the supplier they will probably advise you to take the matter up with the company that holds the service agreement. If the problem is of such a nature that they are unable to help (beyond the conditions of their contract), you then take the problem up with the manufacturer.

If you are lucky they will have a sales office in the UK. Normally the company holding the service agreement should solve your problem but there could be hidden costs. If they operate an on-site warranty they will send out a service engineer to effect repairs on the PC system – you therefore don't incur any costs. If, on the other hand, you have to return the PC you may have to pay delivery costs.

Whatever happens the process is likely to cause quite a lot of inconvenience. However, it is worth remembering that it is almost assured that you will get the repairs or replacement needed eventually.

Getting technical support
It's customary when buying a PC from new to expect some technical support from the supplier or manufacturer. Normally when you make your first enquiry (over the telephone) you will be asked for the equipment serial number and you will be issued with a customer reference number. You are expected to produce this reference for future enquiries. Somewhere in the paperwork there will be a note saying how many hours of free technical support you are entitled to. Each time you require support the duration of your telephone call is metered and docked off your entitlement. Once expired you have to pay.

Checking technical support
There are, however, hidden problems in this scheme. The amount of support a supplier has available at any one time is limited. When you telephone, you may enter a queue which may take as long as 20 minutes. In the meantime, of course, you're paying for the telephone charges and for the privilege of waiting. It's by no means unknown to queue to enter another queue. An alternative worth considering is to send a fax and ask them to ring you back.

Before you buy a PC, it may be a good idea to ring up an intended company and ask to be put through to technical support. You will then be able to judge for yourself whether they offer the prompt technical support that you really want. If the technical support is not as prompt as you consider reasonable you'd be better off going to another supplier.

Buying secondhand

As an investment for a cash product the PC is extremely poor – the depreciation on a PC compares with that of a new car. What is a high performer today will appear to be quite modest by this time next year. This is bad news for the owner trying to get a good price for their 18-month-old PC. As a rule, if you see a secondhand PC for sale, chances are you can buy a new model, with the same capability, for the same price or even less. If you buy secondhand you cannot assume that you have a reliable PC, and if something goes wrong with it you will have to bear the repair costs.

Needing more memory

There is also the problem with new software and its insatiable appetite for memory. If you buy a PC that is twelve months old, it is highly unlikely that it will be fully suitable for running today's software. It will probably not have enough memory and the CPU will probably be too slow to make it viable. If it's already out-of-date just think what it's going to be like in twelve months' time.

Be prepared for upgrading

If you do buy a secondhand PC be prepare to add (or replace) the current RAM and possibly upgrade the CPU. The combined costs of both of these will not make the purchase of a secondhand PC viable anyway. Another disadvantage of buying secondhand is the probable absence of a current warranty. Very few people renew a warranty on a PC that they are about to sell. It may not even be worth renewing the warranty owing to the depreciation already suffered by the PC. Even if you are offered what was a top of the range model two years ago at a bargain price, the question to ask yourself is whether it will fulfil your current and future needs.

WHAT'S EXPECTED OF A PC?

There are two types of users of PC, the new user and the experienced user. Time and practice will change the former into the latter. If you have never used a PC at all or you've had very little experience of using one, bear in mind that you do not need to learn everything about it overnight, and that you will only need to learn about those aspects which you are going to use in the course of your particular application. This may take several weeks, but you will be gaining benefits from your PC right from day one. You will, however, have to be prepared for moments of frustration when it doesn't do what you expect or you are unable to get the PC to do what you want. There will also be occasions when the PC (or one of its peripherals) stops functioning properly without any apparent reason.

Providing fundamental services

Irrespective of your needs the PC will be expected to provide a variety of fundamental services. After all, it should be regarded as a general purpose tool for manipulating information. The common services will be:

- **Wordprocessing** (WP). Needed to create written documents and store them for future reference. There are many quality WP packages on the market (see Chapter 4).

- **Storing data**. There are many ways of storing data on PCs. The data could be written text documents or images (pictures). Alternatively the information could be numerical or lists of items, in which case spreadsheets and databases could be used.

- **Generating presentation material**. This can be accomplished with a suitable presentation software package such as Stamford Graphics – also used for creating slides (see Chapter 4).

- **Generating data tables**. Required to present data in tabular format. Spreadsheets and some modern WP packages perform this task very well.

- **Creating and storing diagrams**. Many theses will have drawings or diagrams in. Drawings can be generated on a PC using a variety of packages. Simple diagrams are quite easy to produce. However, if you require artistic features you will encounter problems. Flexible drawing hardware (pens linked to graphics tablets) are quite expensive. Alternatively, diagrams and pictures can be imported using a scanner or digital camera.

- Accessing the Internet.

- **Performing data manipulation**. Very much the task of a spreadsheet and quite straightforward to use.

Benefits of visual information

The attractive feature of using a PC is the visual aspect which can be gained immediately with the PC graphics screen. Pictures are always more communicative than pages of text or tables of numbers. Fortunately there are many software packages on the market which facilitate the creation of pictorial information.

SELECTING A PC

New PCs have certain features in common:

- **Central processing unit (CPU)**: the microprocessor that executes programs and controls most of the operations in the PC.

- **Motherboard**: the main printed circuit board with the electronics components on including the CPU and the memory chips.

- **Hard-disc unit**: the main data and program storage facility in your PC.

- **Floppy disc drive**: the small drive that you access from the front of your PC – sometimes needed to install new software onto the hard-disc drive.

- **CD-ROM drive**: to accommodate CD-ROMs which are becoming the alternative means of holding data and programs.

- **Display monitor**: the principal interface between the user and the PC by providing visual information.

- **Mouse**: now an essential feature for controlling the operation of programs using the **point and click** technique.

- **Keyboard**: the principal means of controlling the operation of the PC.

- **Interface facilities**: the means to interface external peripherals to the PC – a printer, for example.

There will be a degree of variation in this list depending on the
intended application of the PC. For example, if the PC is intended
for multimedia applications then it will be equipped with a sound
card (see Chapter 3) and two or more external loudspeakers. When
buying a new PC it will probably be necessary for you to consider all
these features in turn and they are discussed in greater detail in
Chapter 2.

The external design of PCs today falls into three categories: desk-
top, tower or lap-top.

Desktop PCs (Figure 1)

These used to be the most common of the three designs. However,
their major problem is the amount of room they take up on the desk
– room that could be put to better use. If you are intending to
augment your system in the future it may be unwise to buy a desk-
top design because of the limited room inside the main unit to add
extra components such as extra disc-drives or expansion cards.
These days the size of the main unit, often referred to as its
footprint, is now standard.

Tower system (Figure 2)

This design has grown in popularity, because, as it is floor standing,
it can be situated under a desk. Three sizes are normally available:
large, mid-tower and mini-tower. Floppy disc drives, CD-ROM
drives, the back-up tape drives and similar peripheral devices all
come in standard sizes and are accommodated in the PC's **5¼inch
bays**. The main difference between each tower size is the number of
bays in each. For example, the mini-tower will probably have two
whereas the mid-tower will have four. In general it has more internal
room for accommodating extra peripherals as required.

Both desktops and tower systems come with screen monitors
which are cathode ray tubes – like a normal television. In general
there is no extra cost when specifying a tower system.

The lap-top (Figure 3)

This design has proved to be very popular. It takes up the least
amount of room and usually has a **liquid crystal display** (LCD)
screen. Although lap-top PCs are very attractive there are a couple
of disadvantages that you should be aware of. Because they are
portable, they have a limited amount of room internally which can
be a problem if you want to add internal peripherals. They are also
battery powered. Although they are rechargeable the operating time

Fig. 1. The desktop PC has traditionally
been the most common configuration.

Fig. 2. Tower designs have become very popular
because they can be stored away under desks.

Fig. 3. The portability of lap-top PCs
makes them very attractive for people on the move.

may be limited to a few hours. There is also a greater risk of losing a lap-top, or having it stolen. Although the PC can be replaced the data on its hard-disc cannot be replaced so easily if back-ups are not kept. Lap-tops usually cost more than the normal desk-top PC but in general they are very convenient to use.

Using a lap-top to communicate with your office
If you are thinking about buying a lap-top PC you may wish to consider a variety of peripherals for remote communication purposes. If your profession entails a lot of travelling and you wish to have a data link with your office you will need a PC with a PCMCIA interface (see Chapter 5). This will allow you to interface your lap-top to a modem and mobile telephone. Information can then be transferred between you and your office with relative ease. However, these add-ons do not come cheap.

Looking at magazines and advertisements
There are many companies selling PCs though mail order and it's a useful and worthwhile exercise to look through a few PC magazines in your local newsagents. You will find that the major PC suppliers have advertisements in all the well-known PC magazines normally occupying several consecutive pages. A list of PC magazines can be found in Appendix B, but note that the list cannot be totally up-to-date and complete because of the rapid emergence and demise of such publications.

CHECKLIST

● Define as tightly as possible what you require from your PC. Do this by drawing up your personal list of needs.

● Allocate a budget for the purchase of a PC. If you are buying it to make money make a realistic assessment of the pay-back time (which should not exceed one year).

● Try and select a supplier that is within easy driving distance of your home.

● Always pay with a credit card, never cash.

CASE STUDIES

Owing to the immense flexibility of the PC, it can be configured for a variety of applications. Naturally one of the constraining features will be cost, therefore in the following case studies we shall consider three applications requiring three PC price bands. In the three case studies the cost of the PC only will be considered – excluding software or peripherals. There may be several items in the specification list that you don't yet know about. You will find additional information in the appropriate sections (Chapters 2, 3, 4 and 5) in this book.

Mary requires a PC for essay and assignment preparation

In most universities and colleges in Britain, submitted essays and assignments are expected to be printed. Although facilities are usually provided within the institution many students prefer to buy their own PC. Because of the poor grant position Mary will find the purchase of a PC a significant load to carry and she may require an additional bank loan. The specifications for a PC to satisfy her needs and the majority of student requirements are:

133 MHz Pentium processor	16 Mbyte RAM
1.2 Gbyte EIDE hard-disc	14 inch NI SVGA colour monitor
Graphics card with 1 Mbyte RAM	8 speed CD-ROM drive
256 kbyte cache memory	Windows 95 or 98
Sound Blaster 16 sound card	2 serial ports and 1 parallel port

Cost £400.

Robert wants a PC for the home

Many a PC is bought for home and domestic purposes which means that it will have several users. Robert has a teenage son who will want to play games and access the Internet, whereas Robert and his wife will want it for letter writing, monitoring the home finances and also accessing the Internet. The specifications of a PC that will satisfy Robert's needs are:

200MHz MMX processor	32 MByte of EDO RAM

2.0 Gbyte Mode-4 hard-disc	15 inch NI SVGA colour monitor
3D Graphic Accelerator card with 4 Mbyte of VRAM	PnP BIOS extension
16 speed CD-ROM drive	Sound Blaster AWE64 Gold
External stereo speakers	2 x 16,550 serial ports
1 parallel port	Windows 95 or 98
512 kbyte burst pipeline cache	Tower design

Cost £1000.

Andrew wants a PC for his small publishing company

The main tasks will be processing text, pictures and images. For this type of application, Andrew's PC will have to be fast and have a lot of memory – both RAM and hard-disc. Images and pictures require a lot of memory and Andrew should make provision to include these items in his basic PC configuration, as well as allowing for more memory at a later date quickly and easily:

233MHz Pentium II processor	Intel 440LX PCIset
64 Mbyte EDO RAM in DIMMs	6.4 Gbyte Wide SCSI Hard-disc drive
17 inch NI SVGA colour monitor	Millennium Mystique 2D Graphics card with 8 Mbyte of VRAM and MPEG decoder
24 speed CD-ROM drive	512 kbyte burst pipeline cache
56 kbps internal FAX/modem	USB Interface extension
Adaptec SCSI-2 adaptor	AWE 64 Gold sound card
Windows 95, 98 or NT	2 x 16,550 serial ports
ATX form-factor motherboard	1-ECP/EPP printer port

Cost £2,500.

DISCUSSION POINTS

1. Make a list of the skills you think you will need in order to make the most of your PC after you have bought it.

2. Look through the *Yellow Pages* and compile a list of PC suppliers within a ten-mile radius (note their fax number). Sending a written specification is preferable to giving one over the telephone as it minimises confusion.

3. Fill in Table 1 of possible current and future applications of your PC. Look out for the peripherals and software discussed further on in the book that may be used when considering new applications for your PC.

2
Understanding the
PC's Components

Before you buy a new PC you should have a reasonable idea of what you are buying, and although a particular model may appear to be attractive from the outside, what really counts is what's inside and the present state of technology. This chapter will therefore provide you with the necessary information to make a judgement on the specifications of most models that you are likely to encounter. You will probably come across terms in this chapter that you have not met before. This is an inevitable consequence of new developing technologies and although a thorough understanding is not always required you will at least appreciate their significance within the context of PC design.

LOOKING INSIDE A PC

Inside the main unit of the PC are a number of components: the disc units, the power supply and the motherboard, which is the printed circuit board on which many of the electronic components are mounted. These days motherboards are very compact with relatively few electronic integrated circuits (chips). There is a battery-powered real-time clock on the motherboard which provides the date and time.

The motherboard's components
Probably you will not have had an opportunity of looking inside the main unit of the PC. When you are buying from new you should, however, be aware of what you are buying as it makes all the difference to the performance of the PC. Although it's not necessary to know the function of all the devices on the motherboard, it always helps to know what role the more important devices play. These include:

- the chipset
- the Basic Input Output System (BIOS)

- CMOS RAM
- the central processing unit – CPU (discussed below).

ATX Motherboard

Many PCs have a specification for the motherboard known as the ATX which has been designed to enable PC manufacturers to produce components cheaply. It has a so-called form-factor which is a reduced size board (Baby-AT) with new mounting features for the new power supply design. The CPU is located well away from the expansion slots but close to the cooling fan on the power supply. The ATX design should allow the integration of more input/output features (serial bus and graphics functions) on the motherboard and should reduce the amount of cabling to disc drives, resulting in lower production costs. It's much easier to assemble a PC with an ATX motherboard owing to the layout of components on the board.

Chipset

The chipset, which comprises one or more integrated circuits, performs all the operational functions relating to data flow between the CPU and the input/output devices and the internal expansion bus. Some chipsets support the universal serial bus (USB) which is likely to be the principal means of enabling communication between the PC and external peripherals. There are a number of chipsets on the market; Intel's designs include:

- **Intel 430VX**. Designed for home and low cost small business PCs which require good multimedia performance. The chipset has the Intel Concurrent PCI architecture which enables the CPU, the PCI and ISA buses to carry data concurrently, thereby allowing smooth video (MPEG) and audio performance to be realised.

- **Intel 430HX**. Designed to be used in higher reliability business PCs where there is a need for constant error checking and enables large RAM areas to be allocated – up to 512 Mbyte. Like the 430VX, the 430HX allows Concurrent PCI giving a potentially high quality multimedia performance. HX also supports USB and is a chipset well matching the operational needs of the Pentium processor. Intel even make a motherboard TC430HX, which not only hosts this chipset but also supports the MMX processor.

- **Intel 430TX**. The TX chipset has been introduced to match the needs of the MMX processor and is likely to be found in battery packed lap-top PCs owing to its power saving facilities (Dynamic Power Management Architecture). Like the 430HX it supports the USB which is particularly appealing to lap-top makers who are considering Plug and Play peripheral interfacing. It also supports the Ultra DMA/33 (direct memory access) for fast hard-disc data transfer and is well matched for the needs of the MMX processor.

- **Intel 440FX**. This chipset has been optimised for the Pentium II and Pentium Pro processors executing 32-bit software and found on PCs in the top end of the range. Based on the Concurrent PCI architecture, it has what is known as a multi-transaction timer (MTT) for enhanced video performance which works together with a passive release mechanism for efficient MPEG and audio processing. The 440FX can be used to access up to 1 Gbyte of EDO RAM if required. It's also suitable for symmetric multiprocessor (SMP) systems hosting two Pentium Pro or Pentium II processors.

- **Intel 440LX PCIset**. This chipset supports the Accelerated Graphics Port (AGP) which in effect is a direct connection between the system RAM and the graphics facility (point-to-point connection). The 440LX PCIset also supports synchronous dynamic RAM (SDRAM) and the Ultra DMA hard-disc drive protocol. It has been designed to optimise the performance of the Pentium II processor. In essence the 440LX chipset facilitates very fast data transfer across the new PCI 2.1 expansion bus which operates at 66 MHz (twice the rate of the standard PCI bus). It accomplishes this by employing techniques known as sideband address and pipelining. It's likely that the 440LX PCIset will be followed by the 440BX.

BIOS

In order to marshal information in and out of the CPU, some control software is required and this resides in the Basic Input Output System (BIOS) memory chips on the motherboard. One famous supplier of this software is **American Megatrends Corporation** (AMC) and when you power up the PC you will see their logo appear on the screen. When you are buying a new PC make sure that the BIOS is **Plug and Play** (PnP) compatible (see Chapter 4), otherwise the full potential of Windows will not be realised. If the

BIOS is PnP compatible you will see this information appear on the monitor as the PC powers up.

CMOS RAM

The information (data) relating to how the PC is configured is stored in the CMOS RAM which draws its power from the battery on the motherboard. Although it is unlikely to affect the new owner, if you make changes to the system, such as adding another disc unit, you will have to change the information in the CMOS RAM. This is achieved by pressing the Del key on the keyboard as the PC is powering up. You should know what you are doing before you attempt any changes yourself.

Sound generation

You will also find on some motherboards all the electronics needed to generate sounds thereby obviating the need to have a sound card – this is normally a cheaper solution. This information will be provided in the specification listing for the PC.

THE CENTRAL PROCESSING UNIT (CPU)

The intelligence of a PC is derived from the host microprocessor, often called the CPU. Every computer program (also known as software) is basically a list of instructions and it's the CPU that executes these instructions. The problem is that there are several different families of CPUs and to make matters even more complicated, members of the same family operate at different speeds.

Intel

On many PC units you will see the little logo **Intel Inside** or **Pentium Inside**. This indicates that the PC has a CPU made by the American microprocessor manufacturer **Intel**. Intel's common CPUs are the 486DX and the Pentium (and their variants). However, there are other manufacturers which make compatible versions that are just as good. Examples of these are **Cyrix** and **AMD**. The **Apple Macs**, on the other hand, use CPUs manufactured by **Motorola** (the MC68000 family). The types of processors operate in quite different ways. This is why Apple Mac programs do not normally run on PCs.

Clock speeds

A rough indication of the speed of a CPU is **clock speed**, measured in Mega Hertz (MHz – millions of cycles per second) and ranging from 20 MHz to in excess of 300 MHz for the more upmarket PCs. When buying a new PC today you should be looking for a clock speed of not less than 90 MHz.

Double speed
Some CPUs operate in a clock double speed mode. This means that the internal clock rate is faster than the clock speed for the rest of the motherboard. The 486DX2 (see below) is an example: the clock speed for the motherboard chips may be 33 MHz but the internal clock speed of the CPU is doubled to 66 MHz. A PC with a 486DX2 will execute most programs faster than a 486DX.

However, the average operating speed is not necessarily doubled since much of a program's execution time requires data transfer from and to RAM and hard-disc which operates at the speed of a 486DX. Generally, the higher the clock speed the more expensive the PC. Just to make life a little more interesting, the 486DX4 CPU has an internal clock speed of 100 MHz.

SELECTING A CPU

When buying a new PC you will have a basic choice of three CPUs. For serious applications your PC should host one of the following:

- **486DX**. When looking at the bottom end of the market you should be thinking of a 486DX with a clock speed of 33 or better still 50 MHz. Slightly better will be a 486DX2 with a clock speed of 66 MHz. You may even find a competitively priced PC with a 100 MHz 486DX4 CPU. Since prices for these older CPUs are now stable you should be able to find a PC hosting one of these CPUs for less than £500.

- **Pentium**. Now the standard CPU for today's PCs. If you intend to run Microsoft's Windows then a Pentium is a must. The 64-bit CPU marks a significant advance in microprocessor development and clock speeds range from 75 MHz to 200 MHz. When first introduced, there was a problem with early batches of Pentium processors with regard to some numerical operations – this was especially true for the 60 MHz versions and was rectified with later versions of the device. It is customary to express the clock speed of the processor in the manner: Pentium P120 – this indicates a 120 MHz Pentium. The Pentium CPU is also compatible with the **K5** from **AMD**, the **Nx586** from **NexGen** and the **6x86** from **Cyrix** – these are all worthy CPUs.

- **Pentium Pro**. Top of the range PCs will host a Pentium Pro CPU (or even two or three). These would be very high performance PCs with clock speeds of 150 to 300 MHz (or even higher) and would serve as very attractive platforms for mathematical modelling and intensive image manipulation operations. They only perform particularly well with software specifically written for a 32-bit CPU.

- **MMX**. Multimedia is becoming an important component in the application of PCs. To achieve effective multimedia performance Intel have produced the MMX processor which is an extended version of the Pentium. Also known as the P55C, the MMX is a variant of the Pentium and has been designed to optimise many operations needed to realise multimedia processes – this is especially true for high intensive graphics applications. It will certainly be an added boost to games applications which make high demands on graphics processing. Although software designed for the Pentium will run on MMX-based PCs, to capitalise on the MMX processor, software must be specifically compiled to run on it and these products will show the MMX logo on their packaging. The MMX is available in a number of clock speeds including 200 MHz, 233 MHz and 266 MHz. As with other processors the higher the clock rate the greater the performance and the higher the cost. It's customary to find the MMX accommodated in what is known as a Socket 7. An alternative to the MMX is the 6x86MX from Cyrix which has a cache of 64 kbyte. Again this promises to be a low cost alternative to Intel's processors.

- **Pentium II**. To cater for future needs Intel have produced this enhanced version of the Pentium. Known as the Pentium II (or Klamath) it's designed to be used in multiprocessor workstations and PCs. It has what is known as a dual independent bus (DIB) architecture: one bus for the Level 2 cache and the other bus for multiple parallel transactions. The Pentium II also incorporates the MMX architectural features and 32 kbyte of Level 1 cache which means that it's very efficient for multimedia and communications applications. It's packaged in a single edge contact (SEC) cartridge whose appearance is quite different from

that of other CPUs. The cartridge also contains 512 kbyte of
Level 2 cache. The SEC connects to the motherboard via Intel's
propriety Slot 1 architecture. Clock speeds for the Pentium II
start at 233 MHz, 266 MHz and exceed 300 MHz, and it's likely
that it will replace the Pentium Pro. PCs which have the Pentium
II will have the following motif on it.

- **AMD-K6**. Advanced Micro Devices (AMD) also make a CPU
  which has a comparable performance to that of the Pentium II
  with enhanced MMX features. The AMD-K6 is a lower cost
  device and several PC manufacturers have adopted it in their PC
  designs. The AMD-K6 is accommodated in a Socket 8 which is
  also used for accommodating the Pentium Pro. This processor is
  available in a variety of clock speeds including 166 MHz, 200
  MHz and 233 MHz.

Previous Intel CPUs

Prior generations of CPUs included the 386, which is now very
dated and you should not really entertain a PC based on this CPU.
By today's standards it's slow and is not well suited for running
Microsoft Windows (see Chapter 5). An early version of the 486
CPU (known as the 486SX) is another CPU to avoid. Although
faster than the 386, it's a reduced version of the 486DX and a lot
slower. By today's standards it is now rather dated.

Pentium Overdrive

It is quite possible to upgrade a high-performing 486-based PC by
replacing the 486DX CPU by a Pentium Overdrive CPU. The
performance will not be as good as standard Pentium. In the long
run it may be worthwhile replacing the whole motherboard with one
designed for a Pentium and a new Pentium CPU.

GETTING TO KNOW YOUR RAM

Before a program (or a piece of software) can run, a copy of the
program must be loaded into the memory that is directly accessible

by the CPU. This memory is known as **Random Access Memory** (RAM) and software is copied into RAM from a mass storage device such as a hard-disc or CD-ROM (see below). On PCs, in the early days (1980s), the maximum amount of usable RAM was 640 kbyte. However, things have changed a lot since then and now RAM is measured in Mbyte. The size of RAM to be found in one of today's PCs may vary between 4 Mbyte and 64 Mbyte (or even more). Certainly the absolute minimum is 8 Mbyte but a more realistic value is 16 Mbyte. But if possible and if you can afford it you should aim for higher quantities than this.

When running **Microsoft Windows** you will generally find that **multitasking** (several programs running at the same time) operations run a lot smoother when there is a large amount of RAM available on your PC. There are some programs whose memory requirement will invariably exceed the available RAM in your PC. This is particularly true for software which manipulates images (for example **Photoshop** from **Adobe**). It is therefore necessary to invoke the **virtual memory** facility in Windows.

Swap or virtual memory

Virtual memory, also known as **swap memory**, in effect makes the hard-disc appear as if it's an extension of RAM. The penalty you pay for using virtual memory is a massive reduction in performance. This can be appreciated by comparing the access times of RAM and hard-disc: RAM can be accessed in less than 100 nsec (0.1 microseconds) whereas the hard-disc will take 12,000 microseconds (0.012 seconds) for every access. In Windows virtual memory is configured automatically for you.

SIMMS

Memory chips (RAM) come in Mbyte blocks, 8, 16, 32 Mbyte (or even larger), and the majority of them are packaged as **single inline memory modules** or SIMMS which usually have 30- or 72-pin edge connectors. The PC's motherboard has an area allocated for the accommodation of SIMMS (usually four white sockets). For a PC with a Pentium processor 72-pin SIMMS always come in pairs. These SIMMS are 32-bit devices whereas the Pentium processor expects 64-bits, hence the pair configuration. If you are about to buy a pair of SIMMS it's recommended that you do not buy anything less than 16 Mbyte.

DIMMS

Dual inline memory modules (DIMMS) are 168-pin devices and have 64-bit data buses to match the needs of the Pentium processor, hence they come singly. You have to ensure that the motherboard has DIMM sockets to accommodate the 168-pin devices. Typically the access time for a DIMM should be 60 nsec (or less) to support a 200 MHz processor. You may also come across a specification regarding data buffering (buffered or unbuffered) with various voltage options: ensure all the DIMMS are compatible.

SIMMs and parity

You will also find that SIMMs come with a **parity** option. This relates to an error-checking mechanism. In general SIMMs with **full parity** are more expensive. On very rare occasions faults occur in SIMMs and if you are concerned with this potential problem you should specify full parity as opposed to the non parity option. If you do increase the amount of RAM make sure that you consult the User's Manual which comes with your PC. It should also indicate whether SIMMs with parity checking are accepted.

EDO-RAM

There is a variety of RAM known as **extended data out (EDO-RAM)** that has an advantage over conventional RAM: it's faster because it's able to start a new memory access cycle before the previous one has been completed. If possible you should try and specify EDO-RAM when buying a new PC.

SDRAM

There is yet a faster type of RAM available, known as **synchronous dynamic RAM** (SDRAM) which enhances data transfer through the PCI bus. This enables faster communication between the CPU and the expansion cards thus giving an edge on graphics performance. SDRAM works very efficiently with the MMX processor to optimise graphics performance and by facilitating high quality digital video on the PC. There are four aspects to SDRAM which help in its performance:

- Data transfer is clocked to and from SDRAM to ensure synchronous operation, other types of RAM are of an asynchronous nature and require extra control signals.

- Cell Banks for pipelining – dividing the SDRAM into separately addressable cell banks allows data to be transferred during one cycle while simultaneous addressing goes on for the next cycle.

- Burst mode data transfer for effecting efficient direct memory access (DMA).

- Command Mode Storage Registers – by writing command words to these registers the CPU can configure the SDRAM to perform in the above modes; the operation of the memory can therefore be controlled to suit whatever application.

Cache memory
Cache memory resides between the main system RAM and the CPU and has the effect of improving the execution speed of programs. The access time of the cache memory is much shorter than the main RAM. When a segment of program is fetched from the RAM a copy of it is made in cache. When the same segment is required again, instead of fetching it from RAM it is fetched from the cache memory which is much quicker than RAM. The overall result is faster program execution.

The 486, Pentium and MMX processors have a small amount of on-board cache (often called Level 1 cache) of its own. However, this is normally supplemented by an additional external amount (called Level 2 cache). Cache memory in PCs are integrated circuits which reside on the motherboard not too far away from the CPU. Typically you would expect to find either 256 kbyte or 512 kbyte of cache in a new PC.

Burst mode pipeline cache
If you are intending to buy a PC with a Pentium CPU make sure that it has a minimum of 256 kbyte of burst mode pipeline cache. You will also find, on new motherboards, close to the CPU, a slot for accommodating extra cache – known as **coast** (cache on a stick) which is a means of expanding the amount of external cache memory for the CPU.

LOOKING AT HARD-DISC DRIVES

Memory is a very important consideration in the purchase of a PC. **You can never have too much memory**. What you can have, and is very often the case, is too little memory. What may appear to be adequate memory today will be too little tomorrow. This has always been true, right through the history of computers. Memory needs change from year to year depending on the nature of the commercial software used on the PC.

Understanding hard-disc design

A fundamental component that is required in all PCs is the hard-disc drive – where the programs and data are stored. It is basically a stack of rotating platters with a set of reading/writing heads which move over the platter surfaces. The data is stored in the magnetic coating on the platters.

Tracks, sectors and cylinders

Each platter is partitioned into circular tracks and each track is in turn partitioned into individual sectors where the data resides. With several platters forming a stack, you can think of the vertical tracks as a cylinder. Therefore to locate a piece of data all that is needed is the platter number, the cylinder number and the sector number – these three values form a coordinate. It's quite possible to have tracks that are damaged. The electronics on the hard-disc drive ensures that the damaged tracks are never used. Normally the number of damaged tracks is very small and does not affect the performance of the unit.

Boot-sector

The hard-disc drive has on it a **boot-sector** and a **directory**. When the PC is first powered up an **operating system** must be loaded into the CPU's memory and this comes from the boot-sector. The directory is a list of the data and program files held on the disc. Current hard-discs have circuitry which senses a power loss and the heads are locked automatically over a part of the platters that are empty. When buying a new PC the hard-disc drive will be a standard component.

IDE and EIDE

The minimum standard you should look for in a hard-disc drive is one that conforms to the **integrated drive electronics** (IDE) design (see Figure 4) also known as the **Advanced Technology Attachment** (ATA) which is industry standard for hardware connections. AT was the name given to IBM's second generation of PCs made in the mid-1980s. IDE indicates that all the control electronics are built into the drive unit itself. The consequence of this design is a less complex disc controller which normally takes the form of an expansion card (see below) resident in the PC.

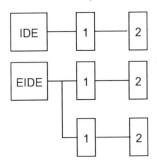

Fig. 4. IDE and EIDE standards for hard-disc interfacings.
IDE supports two devices, master 1 and slave 2, whereas
EIDE supports four devices, two masters and two slaves.

If there is a disc controller expansion card it will also be needed
for the floppy disc drive. The maximum hard-disc size for an IDE
drive is 540 Mbyte and the data transfer rates of an IDE drive range
from 625 kbyte to 2 Mbyte per second. This amount of memory is
far too small for today's requirements and the **enhanced integrated
drive electronics** (EIDE) was introduced to overcome this problem
(see Figure 4). The EIDE specifications also include an updated
version of ATA, called the **ATA packet interface** (ATAPI) which you
may see referred to on hard-disc units.

EIDE and the CD-ROM drive
The EIDE also recognises the CD-ROMs. It is customary to have a
direct connection between the EIDE drive(s) and the motherboard
owing to the disc controller being an integral component on the
motherboard. With the EIDE it's possible to have four hard-disc
drives – Primary Master, Primary Slave, Secondary Master and
Secondary Slave. When the PC is powered up you will see the disc
configuration on the opening banner along with the processor type
and clock speed.

Buying a large enough hard-disc
Hard-disc drives are available in various sizes ranging from 40
Mbyte at the bottom end (earlier devices are smaller but are not
adequate for today's needs) up to several Gbyte (1,000 Mbyte).
When buying from new or upgrading your current PC you should go
for the largest you can afford. 200 Mbyte will probably prove to be

too small within a few months. You should realistically be looking at a minimum of 850 Mbyte for a hard-disc drive. At the time of writing a 2.2 Gbyte hard-disc costs £150. Also bear in mind that if you have a desk-top or tower design PC then you will be able to add other hard-disc units at a later date if required.

Reliability of hard-discs

As the technology of hard-disc drives has advanced, so has their reliability. Typically the mean time before failure (MTBF) will be between 300,000 and 500,000 hours. Provided the PC is treated with respect, the hard-disc should give you trouble-free service. However, the once common **disc crash** can still happen as a result of mechanical breakdown and you are advised to keep a back-up of the data and software on your hard-disc drive.

Hard-disc modes

When specifying a hard-disc drive you may come across a reference to **modes**. The **peripheral input output** (PIO) standard refers to the manner in which data is transferred from the hard-disc to the system RAM. Mode 3 supports data transfer of 11.1 MBits/sec whereas Mode 4 supports a rate of 16.6 Mbits/sec.

Alternatively data can be transferred directly between the hard-disc and RAM without the intervention of the CPU using **direct memory access** (DMA). Multiword DMA Mode 1 and Mode 2 have respective rates of 13.3 Mbits/sec and 16.6 Mbits/sec. Sometimes you may see other specifications of the type:

- **Fast ATAPI**, support for PIO Mode 3 with Multiword DMA Mode 1.

- **Fast ATAPI-2**, support for PIO Mode 4 with Multiword Mode 2.

In some applications you may need to maximise the data transfer rate – performing image manipulation operations, for example. You should therefore look for these standards. The fastest EIDE hard-discs will conform to PIO Mode 4.

Disc caching

Quite often you will see a mention of disc caching. This is a small amount of memory set aside to help maximise the data transfer rate between the hard-disc and the RAM. It is usually a software process and is quite transparent to users of Windows. However, users of older versions of Windows (3.1 or 3.11) will be aware of a disc caching software utility known as **smartdrive**.

Ultra DMA Hard-disc Protocol

Direct memory access (DMA) is a process by which data is transferred between a hard-disc drive and the system RAM without the involvement of the CPU. Ultra DMA is a protocol for EIDE hard discs which enables a burst transfer rate of 33 Mbyte per second to be performed. Patented by the Quantum Corporation (a major manufacturer of hard-disc drives), the protocol is implemented in a number of Intel chipsets including the 430TX series. To realise Ultra DMA a PC will require an appropriate chipset (or a compatible PCI adapter card), a compatible BIOS, an Ultra DMA-aware software driver and a hard-disc (or CD-ROM) device which is also compatible. The overall effect of having Ultra DMA is greater data transfer rates from your hard-disc, a necessary feature if you are manipulating a lot of images with your PC.

SCSI

An alternative to EIDE is the **Small Computer System Interface** (SCSI) design (see Figure 5). SCSI normally requires a dedicated expansion card (probably manufactured by Adaptec) that can be accessed not only by the internal hard-disc drives but also by additional external drives and peripherals.

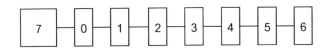

Fig. 5. The SCSI chain of peripherals.
The SCSI host is No. 7, seven peripherals can be cascaded in a chain each having their own identification number between 0 and 6.

The principal benefit of the SCSI design is the option of easily increasing storage capacity by adding external and internal disc-drives. SCSI also affords very fast data transfer rates. Another advantage of the SCSI design is the ability to **daisy chain** other peripherals, such as tape back-up, to the same SCSI controller. This design frees up the CPU from the actual task of data transfer which enables it to get on with other tasks. SCSI comes in a number of varieties:

- **SCSI or SCSI-1**. The first SCSI standard for asynchronous data flow between devices, this meant that the data transfer rate would vary from device to device. In general it reached a data transfer rate of 2 Mbit/s over an 8-bit bus.

- **SCSI-2**. A synchronous data transfer standard with a fixed transfer rate of 5 Mbit/s across an 8-bit bus. Packets of data would transfer between devices where the packet size would be negotiated by the devices. SCSI-2 has become very popular in many PC systems which are used in business environments. A SCSI-2 expansion card will be required to realise this standard; an example is the **Adaptec** AHA-2740W.

- **Fast SCSI-2**. The same as SCSI-2 with the data transfer rate doubled to 10 Mbit/s.

- **Wide SCSI**. The same principles as with the Fast SCSI-2 except data is transferred across a 16-bit bus giving a data transfer rate of 20 Mbit/s. It also required two cables for each device and is rarely used today.

- **Fast-wide SCI-3**. In this standard the connector consists of 68-pins and allows connections between devices with either narrow or wide data channel.

- **Ultra SCSI**. Has the same specification as the SCSI-3 and operates at 20 Mbit/s along a narrow channel.

- **Ultra Wide SCSI**. The Ultra Wide SCSI on the other hand provides a data transfer rate of up to 40 Mbyte/sec and is able to connect up to 15 SCSI peripheral devices. UW-SCSI would normally be used in network servers and workstations, however it's found in some PCs. With four devices on the bus the maximum cable length should not exceed 3 metres. However if there are eight devices the cable length is limited to 1.5 metres. To enable UW-SCSI the PC will require an appropriate SCSI expansion card such as the **Adaptec** AHA-2940UW which provides PCI-to-SCSI. It comes with EZ-SCSI software needed for the installation of the card. If used with the SCSI hard-disc, to realise the full transfer potential you must ensure that the hard-disc is capable of operating at 40 Mbyte/sec.

Hard-discs mostly come with either an EIDE or a SCSI interface, the latter being somewhat more expensive.

Access times

Another feature of the hard-disc drive which affects its performance is its access time (the smaller the better). This is the average time taken for the reading heads to find the required memory location on the platter's surface and transfer the data. This figure should be less than 18 ms (0.018 seconds), and ideally of the order of 9 ms (0.009 seconds) – see the section above on PIO Modes. In general the larger the storage capacity of a hard-disc drive the shorter its access time. Incidentally, you will find that when buying a new PC, the hard-disc drive will already be formatted with the latest version of MS-DOS on it, unless, of course, it comes with Windows which doesn't need MS-DOS. There will, however, still be a version of MS-DOS on the hard-disc.

CHOOSING A FLOPPY DISC DRIVE

Floppy disc drives usually come in two physical sizes, the 5.25 inch and the 3.5 inch. The larger 5.25 version has fallen out of fashion and today most PCs come with a single 3.5 inch drive. The 3.5 inch discs normally come in two capacity sizes, 720 kbyte and 1.44 Mbyte – the latter carrying the high density label (HD). When buying floppy discs it is recommended that you always buy the high density 1.44 Mbyte version. You should back-up your work as a matter of course and floppy discs are useful for this purpose especially if you don't possess a tape drive.

LS120

You may find that some PCs have an alternative to a standard floppy disc drive, a LS120 for super floppies. Having 120Mbyte capacity it's a great improvement on the standard 1.44 Mbyte with the added bonus of being able to read 3.5 inch floppy discs. LS120s, unlike some Zip drives which may need a SCSI expansion card, are ATAPI devices and can be linked to an EIDE channel on the motherboard. You will also find that a LS120 has jumpers to configure it as a master or slave (see section on hard-disc drives). However the LS120 can only be used as boot drive A: provided the BIOS recognises it. Also, only the later versions of Windows 95 come with LS120 driver software.

CHOOSING A CD-ROM DRIVE

The Compact Disc ROM (CD-ROM) drive has become an important peripheral component in a PC. Nearly all vendors supply a CD-ROM drive as standard in their PCs. Since the CD started its commercial life in the audio hi-fi market, moves have been made to extend its format to include the needs of the PC industry. As a result, today CD-ROMS can carry text, images, video, sound, audio and any other relevant data format. In Chapter 3 the standards laid out in the set of Colour Books are discussed.

CD-ROM drive speeds
There are many CD-ROM drives available and broadly speaking they all perform in a similar manner – some a little faster than others. The **single speed** transfer rate is 150 kbits per second. However, when buying a new PC today you should specify nothing less than a **10 speed** CD-ROM (1,500 kbits per second), although sixteen speed (16x) CD-ROMs are becoming standard as indeed 25x speed is increasing in popularity. The CD-ROM has the same basic design as the audio CD and will therefore play audio CDs. All drives have a jack socket on the front for plugging in earphones. You can therefore listen to your favourite music as you are working on the PC, although earphones do get rather uncomfortable after a while.

CD-ROM software driver – MSCDEX
If you buy a PC with Windows 3.11 preloaded (not Windows 95 or 98) you will find a software driver utility to enable the CD-ROM to work. The driver (mscdex.exe – Microsoft CD extension) is loaded when the PC is powered up. This utility is not needed when using Windows 95 or 98.

Storing information
There are several features which make the CD-ROM an attractive medium for carrying information. However, their primary attraction is their storage capacity. A single 5-inch CD-ROM can store up to 660 Mbyte of information. To get some feel of what this means: a full screen SGVA (see section on monitors below) colour image will require 1.4 Mbyte of storage and with image compression, this can be reduced by 40 per cent. Alternatively, in terms of 200-page paperbacks, a CD-ROM can store over 1,300 of them. The stored information can be images, text, software or data and the CD-ROM is treated like any other disc drive. The information is therefore stored

in files that are located in directories (or folders when using Windows) like a normal disc.

DVD-ROM

An alternative to the CD-ROM is the **digital versatile disc** ROM (DVD-ROM) which has a far greater storage capacity than the normal CD-ROM. In fact a DVD can have four storage layers, two per side, and each layer can store over 4.7 Gbyte giving a potential storage of 18.8 Gbyte per disc. With this capacity full length feature films can be easily stored and played back provided the PC is fitted with the appropriate multimedia facilities. Most DVD drives are backward compatible and will read ordinary CD-ROMs. To capitalise on the full potential of a DVD facility you will need an MPEG decoder attached to your graphics card, although in some instances a software MPEG routine may be adequate. An example of a DVD drive is the GD-1000 from **Hitachi** (Tel: (01628) 585490) which uses the MPEG-2 standard for data compression. There are four compatible variants of DVD discs:

- SD-5, single sided, single layer – storage capacity of 4.7 Gbyte
- SD-9, single sided, dual layer – storage capacity of 8.5 Gbyte
- SD-10, dual sided, single layer – storage capacity of 9.4 Gbyte
- SD-18, dual sided, dual layer – storage capacity of 17 Gbyte.

The running time is about 135 minutes per side and S-video footage on DVD will also carry Surround Sound AC-3 encoding which will make it ideal for home entertainment on a grand scale.

Read only

What may be considered a problem is the fact that CD-ROMs are read-only devices. However, it's important to remember that the information stored on a CD-ROM belongs to someone else and, as a user, you are entitled to access it but not to modify its contents on the disc. It is therefore used strictly as a reference source. You are at liberty to generate your own CD-ROMs and this can be done with surprising ease (see Chapter 5 for information on CD-Rs).

Using photographs

A service offered by high street photo development shops is the Kodak Photo CD. You take your photographs in and can then have them transferred onto a CD-ROM. By using the **Kodak Photo CD Access Plus Software** (available on a CD-ROM) you can view and manipulate your images on your PC. If you wish to store text, one way would be to photograph the source page and thereafter treat it like an image. In Chapter 5 there is a discussion on how to retrieve text from an image using **Optical Character Recognition** (OCR) software.

Buying commercial CD-ROMs

When you buy new software you will probably have it supplied on a CD-ROM. Installing software from a CD-ROM is much faster and easier than using floppy discs. If you have the option, request a CD-ROM version. Many applications of the PC involve the access of data or information from various sources, ranging from encyclopaedias to census information. CD-ROM is therefore becoming one of the principal means of storing and accessing information, whether as text, video, images or sound. The CD-ROM is having tremendous success in the games and entertainment market, all part of the multimedia explosion. Microsoft, for example, offer a range of CD-ROM titles on classical music, bird life, mammals and general information. A number of companies specialise in the production of CD-ROMs which carry information relating to a wide range of subjects – Chadwyck-Healey of Cambridge is a prime example.

CHOOSING A MONITOR

With the continual improvements in the manufacturing techniques of cathode ray tubes, screen monitors for PCs have come down in price and have improved in quality. Although there are many manufacturers of monitors, there are established standards for the graphics.

Monitor sizes

Monitors range in size from 14-inch to 21-inch (and possibly larger). The larger the monitor the more expensive it is. When selecting a monitor you should choose the largest you can afford – the larger it is the less strain on the eyes. A large monitor (17-inch) is a must if you intend to spend a lot of time manipulating images of any kind. Although monochrome monitors are available you would be strongly advised to choose the colour option since the additional cost is so marginal and the colour has so much more to offer.

Monitor cables

Two cables normally connect to the monitor, one carrying the mains power and the other carrying the signals. The mains cable will probably connect directly to the back of the PC so that when the power to the PC is switched off the monitor power will switch off as well. The signal cable will have a D-connector with three rows of pins (some missing) and this connects into the graphic expansion card (accessed at the back of the PC).

Graphics standards

Although there have been several graphics standards developed over the past ten years, you should aim for a monitor which supports the SVGA (Super Video Graphics Array) standards. It is the graphics expansion card (see Figure 6) in the PC which actually defines the operating standard. SVGA can operate in several modes depending on the number of dots or **pixels** (picture elements) that are addressed on the monitor. The density of dots is known as the **dot pitch** and measured in mm. You should be looking for a dot pitch of 0.3 mm or less with medium short persistence. The ordinary VGA standard is 640 x 480 dots with 16 colours which is wholly inadequate for today's software and you should ensure that the monitor is of an SVGA design. The SVGA standards include:

- 800 x 600 dots
- 1,024 x 760 dots
- 1,280 x 1,024 dots.

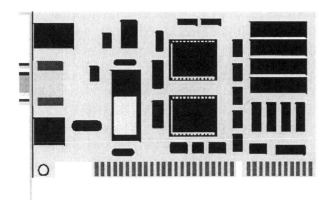

Fig. 6. A graphics expansion card, which has a D-connector on the back panel (left hand side) to link with the monitor cable. The base of the card fits into one of the expansion slots in the PC.

When operating an SVGA 14-inch monitor at 1,024 x 760 or above the images are rather cramped and it becomes difficult to use. For a 14-inch monitor the optimum is 800 x 600 whereas a 17-inch monitor can comfortably cope with a resolution of 1,024 x 760.

Screen refresh frequency
The vertical refresh frequency is important and your monitor should support frequencies in the range 50 to 90 Hz (number of refreshes per second). It is the graphics card that performs the refresh but the monitor must be compatible. The lower the frequency the greater the effect of flicker which can be annoying for long exposure. As you increase the resolution and the number of colours, the refresh rate decreases. You will be able to alter the graphics settings through software. For example, with Windows in the control panel you have the option of selecting the required SGVA mode.

You will often come across the abbreviation **NI** which is short for non-interlaced. This refers to the manner in which the electron beam in the cathode ray tube (CRT) sweeps across the matrix of phosphor dots on the screen (when the electrons strike the phosphor dots they give off light). Normally the beam scans a row of dots, flies back and scans the next row. The refresh frequency is the number of times the beam scans the screen per second. In the design of early monitors the beam would scan the odd rows first, fly back to the start and scan the even rows – this was referred to as interlacing. This had the effect of reducing the quality of the screen image. In modern monitors this should not happen (non-interlaced – NI) except in exceptional cases for large monitors operating at a very high resolution. The rule is, when buying, make sure the monitor is NI.

Green monitor
The monitor should also have a provision for saving energy – known as a green monitor. If required it should be possible to have the monitor power down after a set period of inactivity. You will see the energy saving symbol in the top right-hand corner when the PC is powered up.

Graphics cards
When choosing a new PC it's likely that it will have a PCI bus (see below) and a graphics card (see Figure 6) that occupies one of the PCI slots. Do not buy a PC with an ISA graphics card, it will be too slow for today's software. There will be a graphics engine IC on

board that performs the image housekeeping and a currently popular one is the **S3**. You will frequently see this one specified. Ideally you should be looking for a graphics card that hosts a graphics processor with a 64-bit data path through a PCI bus (see below).

There are four features that you should consider when specifying a graphics card:

- resolution
- colour depth
- on-board memory
- virtual screen.

Resolution
Each dot in a graphics image is known as a **pixel** (picture element) and requires a certain amount of memory. The graphics card should match the requirements of the SVGA monitor by providing a minimum of 1,024 x 760 pixels. The greater the density of pixels the better the resolution. The pixel resolution can be switched through software to obtain the desired image quality. If you are likely to use old software there is a possibility that it will require past standards in graphics resolution. A modern graphics card will automatically switch to the required resolution.

Colour depth
A very important consideration is the range of colours that the graphics card can produce. The current range is 256, 32,768, 65,536 and 16.7 million colours. The greater the number of colours the greater the colour depth. When viewing colour pictures the human eye can distinguish between a screen image made from 65,536 colours and one made from 16.7 million colours.

Each dot on the monitor is made up of three individual primary colours (red, green and blue). For maximum colour depth each colour in each pixel will have a byte of memory allocated to it. A byte, with its 8 bits, gives 256 (2^8 = 256) shades. With three primary colours you will have 256 x 256 x 256 possible colours giving 16.7 million. This is known as 24-bit colour depth (8-bits for each primary colour). If there is not enough memory on the graphics card you may have to sacrifice colour depth for resolution. You will often come across colour ratings, these are high colour (16-bit) and true colour (24-bit and sometimes 32-bit). The greater the colour depth the better the colour quality.

On-board graphics memory

The memory of the graphics card must be sufficient to hold one screen of image data. There is a trade-off. The greater the colour depth and the higher the resolution the greater the amount of memory needed. If you haven't got the memory and you want the resolution you will have to sacrifice the colour depth. If you are running a monitor with a resolution of 1,024 x 760 and you want a colour depth of 16.7 million you will require just over 4 Mbyte of RAM on the graphics card. To maximise the image data throughput you should specify **video RAM** or VRAM. VRAM is fast owing to its separate input and output buses. It has a parallel input bus (from the CPU) and a serial output bus to the monitor.

You should have at least 4 Mbyte of RAM on your graphics card, or better still 8 Mbyte and if you can afford it VRAM. This will maximise image data throughput and give faster graphics.

Virtual screen

Some graphics cards operate a **virtual screen**; for example, the screen image could be 1,024 x 1,536 pixels but only a portion of the image will actually be on the screen. As you move the mouse around the screen the other portions of the image come into view. It's all a matter of taste as to whether you like this type of thing.

Incidentally, if you are thinking of running video proper you will need an MPEG video card (see Chapter 3) to work alongside your graphics card. However, some graphics cards have an MPEG playback facility as part of the design – check the specifications. An example of a well-known graphics card is the **Diamond Stealth 64-bit** with the S3 graphics processor which is supported by 4 or 8 Mbyte of VRAM.

3D accelerator graphics cards

If your PC is likely to be used for playing a lot of games then it may be worthwhile considering a graphics card specifically designed to enable fast action-packed graphics. Collectively known as 3-dimensional (3D) graphics cards, they produce realistic 3D-looking scenes by using a variety of techniques which are realised by means of a **multimedia graphics accelerator processor**. The majority of games scenes are made up of connected polygons which must blend at the edges to give a good sense of realism. Some of the processes for achieving this realism and for accelerating the graphics include:

- **Anti-aliasing**, removal of jagged lines from edges. Extra lines are added to give the impression of softer edges.

- **Shading**, performing the appropriate degree of shading on solid surfaces. **Gouraud shading** is often used, which calculates the amount of light falling on and reflected from surfaces.

- **Texture mapping**, the removal of distortion as a pattern is wrapped around a surface. For example, ensuring that the reflections from a metallic sphere appear even.

- **Quadratic Texture Mapping (QTM)**, an algorithm implemented on some multimedia processors for realising fast texture mapping – improves graphics speed.

- **Z-sorting**, a method for drawing scenes where only the visible surfaces are actually drawn. Since only one view is visible at any one time, only the image data for that view is actually processed – improves graphics speed.

A typical commercial CD graphics card that performs the above operations is the **Diamond Edge 3D 3240XL** which hosts the NV1 multimedia processor.

UNDERSTANDING PC EXPANSION CARDS

One of the features which has contributed to the success of the PC is the option of adding internal peripherals. These are normally connected to the PC system via a set of expansion slots which are situated towards the back of the main PC unit. On a typical motherboard (the printed circuit board bearing most of the electronic devices) of a desk-top PC there should be at least eight expansion slots. However, there are a number of standards which you must be aware of if you are buying from new.

- **ISA** (Industry Standard Architecture). This is the most common and the motherboard of every desk-top and tower PC will have a number of 16-bit ISA slots (also known as the AT bus). There may even be 8-bit ISA slots (identified as half the size of the 16-bit slots) which indicates a poor deal – there really is no reason for having 8-bit ISA slots since all 8-bit ISA expansion cards can be accommodated in 16-bit ISA slots.

- **PCI** (Peripheral Component Interconnect). A bus proposed by

Intel and found in most PCs manufactured today. PCI cards should also be compatible with the PowerPC from Apple and other computer manufacturers. PCI is designed to accommodate 32-bit and 64-bit data transfer and forms part of the strategy for enabling fast video graphics. The maximum data transfer rate is 120Mbit/sec sustained or 132 Mbit/sec in a burst mode. PCI is essential for quality video on a PC.

There are older standards that you should avoid: the **Micro Channel Architecture** (MCA) from IBM and the **Extended Industry Standard Architecture** (EISA). Both of these have been broadly superseded by the PCI bus.

SCSI expansion card adaptors
In the section on hard-disc drives the importance of SCSI (Small Computer System Interface) was discussed. If you are thinking about this option you will probably consider the products made by **Adaptec**. Two examples of their expansion cards are: for ISA to SCSI (AHA-1540) and for PCI to SCSI (AHA-2940).

Famous PC makers
The PC marketplace is highly competitive and this has driven prices down over the past few years. There are many models available and price is not necessarily an indicator of quality. As with other market commodities there are brand leaders like **Compaq**, **Hewlett Packard**, **Dell**, **Apricot**, **Red Box**, **Viglen**, **Packard Bell**, **Olivetti** and of course **IBM**. However, many PCs and their components are sourced in Pacific Rim Nations (Taiwan, for example), are of extremely high quality, and are likely to give you trouble-free service. To gain a feel for what's available for the budget you've allocated for the PC, refer to some of the PC magazines which are currently sold in profusion (see Appendix B).

USING THE KEYBOARD AND THE MOUSE

Much of the user's time will be spent entering information into the PC via the keyboard. Although most keyboards have a standard 102 key format it's always a good idea to try out a keyboard before you buy it. The action of the keys will be important especially if you are a writer and are expecting to spend a few hours every day on your PC. The action varies from being very spongy to very hard or just very tinny.

After several months you may find that your keyboard becomes stained through constant use. You are advised not to try and clean it with any solvent as this is likely to leak down between the keys and damage the contacts. If it's still under warranty you may be able to have it cleaned by the holders of the service contract (see Chapter 1).

Natural keyboards

Unfortunately the standard keyboard is ergonomically unsound and excessive use has led to the now infamous **repetitive strain injury** (RSI). To help eliminate this potential hazard Microsoft and other manufacturers have produced so-called **natural keyboards**. As well as redesigning the shape of the keyboard with split and tilted sections, many shortcut methods are provided through the use of **IntelliType** software.

The mouse

The mouse controls the movement of the screen cursor and the features offered by Windows are all accessed by the mouse via the **click and drag** technique. To use Windows efficiently and any other software package that runs under Windows, a mouse is essential. Many application programs running under Windows will have an interactive element with them and it's commonplace to use the mouse as the interactive tool. This is especially true for learning tutorials on new software packages. There are alternatives to the mouse such as a **tracker ball** but the principle is the same.

Connecting the mouse to the PC
The mouse cable, with its 9-pin D-connector, normally plugs into a serial port (COM1). However, optically coupled mice are available. A mouse driver (a piece of software) will be required although Windows 95 and 98 comes with its own driver. Some PCs have a dedicated round socket to accommodate the mouse connector, although the majority of mice come with the 9-pin D-connector. A mouse normally comes as a standard item when you buy a new PC and is often referred to as **Microsoft mouse compatible**. Incidentally, some mice are designed for either left-hand or right-hand usage.

CHECKLIST

• You can use the information in this chapter to clarify the meaning of specifications found in advertisements for PCs.

- You may, from time to time, have to refer to the section on PC buses. Ideally you should be looking for a PCI bus whatever your price range.

- You should now appreciate the significance of the different types of memory found on PCs: RAM, hard-discs, floppy discs, CD-ROMS and cache.

- If you are likely to spend even a few hours a day working on your PC then you will find that speed is important.

CASE STUDIES

Alan needs a PC system to produce catalogues

Alan has set up his own part-time business producing sales catalogues for small companies. He will need to compile sales information, which will change month by month, to update catalogues. Once information has been collected from the companies relating to what's new, what's existing stock and what's deleted stock, he will need to maintain a current stock list. The hardware requirements for Alan's task are not too demanding. Typically he will need:

- Pentium P166 PC
- 1.2 Gbyte hard-disc
- 16 Mbyte of RAM
- colour 14-inch SVGA monitor
- mouse
- laser printer (see Chapter 5).

When it comes to software all his requirements can be met by using a standard **integrated office suite** (IOS – see Chapter 4) running under Windows. The main features of IOS that will be of interest to Alan are the database to maintain a current record of each company's goods and the wordprocessor to generate the catalogues. One of the attractive features of an IOS is the ability to copy objects, in this case product lists, from one application to another with complete ease. There is also provision within an IOS to cope with pictures if the future need arises.

Bob wants a PC for desktop publishing

The majority of PCs sold today will be used to some extent for producing written documents. The wordprocessor is essential on all PCs, whereas a DTP facility will be needed only if Bob is hoping to prepare documents for mass publication. It must be stressed that many wordprocessors already have several integral DTP features (see Chapter 4 for details of wordprocessor and DTP software). For DTP applications, a Pentium-based PC should be considered. Other hardware requirements are:

- 32 Mbyte of RAM.

- 15-inch monitor: DTP software tends to use document paragraphs as objects that you move around the page. Having a 15-inch monitor improves the viewing resolution and allows you to see things in greater detail.

- 3.0 Gbyte hard-disc: documents with images and pictures take large amounts of storage space and Bob will require a large hard-disc for this purpose.

One additional hardware requirement when dealing with large documents is a back-up facility. Floppy discs are not suitable for this purpose and in Chapter 5, back-up peripherals are discussed in some detail.

Sandra wants to construct a database of customers and suppliers

One of the most powerful aspects of the PC is its ability to store vast amounts of information. However, information by itself is not particularly useful unless you have an effective means of accessing it quickly. Sandra knows that a database is the ideal means for storing similar units of information such as a list of her suppliers and customers. With a database, Sandra has several means of interrogating the stored information. For example, if she wants a partial list of all suppliers that supplied her with goods between two specified dates, this can be done very easily with a database. Fortunately the use of databases on today's PCs is not hardware intensive and standard systems are able to perform database operations with ease. Typical hardware and software would be:

- Pentium P133 PC.
- 2.2 GByte hard-disc (mode 4) with fast access time (less than 12 msec). Database searching tends to be disc-activity intensive and

a short access time is therefore important.
- 32Mbyte of RAM.
- Suitable database software such as Microsoft's Access (see Chapter 4 and Appendix A).

DISCUSSION POINTS

Having gained an appreciation of what to look for inside a new PC unit, it will be worthwhile considering other aspects of interest when specifying a new PC.

1. There will be a substantial depreciation on your PC over the next two years (more than 50 per cent). In view of the capital outlay, make a points list justifying your initial budget and modify it as you consider appropriate.

2. Make a points list justifying the purchase of a Pentium II based PC over that of a MMX PC – is it really cost effective to buy a Pentium II PC?

3
Buying a Multimedia PC

Over the past few years there has been a substantial growth in what is known as the **multimedia** sector. This is a combination of image, text, video, music and sound where the CD-ROM plays the central role for information storage. The key feature of multimedia is user interaction. The phrase **random access** will often arise, meaning that any part of the stored information can be accessed directly. The use of the word 'random' is misleading, since what is really meant is direct access. In effect, it's possible to move very quickly from one piece of information to another, unlike a video tape, for example, where you have to fast forward or rewind until you reach the part of the tape you want.

As mentioned in Chapter 2, Intel have produced the MMX processor which has been optimised for speeding up multimedia applications. If you are involved in the development of multimedia products it would be wise for you to consider the MMX option. Also look out for multimedia software which is MMX compliant.

CREATING MULTIMEDIA MATERIAL

Multimedia material is relatively straightforward to create. Generating your own video footage, sound files and images is by no means difficult. Integrating these into a workable multimedia format is an exciting application of a PC and is an activity pursued by many people. When creating multimedia applications it is customary, but not essential, to use multimedia authoring software and this is covered in detail in Chapter 4.

MULTIMEDIA PC STANDARDS

There are three classifications for PC which conform to the **Multimedia PC Council** standard: MPC, MPC2 and MPC3. MPC is out of date and only MPC2 and MPC3 will be of interest. The

Table 2. MPC2 specifications.

Minimum PC specification	4 Mbyte RAM, 33 MHz 486DX, 200 Mbyte hard-disc
CD-ROM drive	Single speed, CD-ROM XA, multi-session
Audio	16-bit digital sound, MIDI playback
Graphics	1.2 Mega pixels per second

Table 3. MPC3 specifications

Minimum PC specification	8 Mbyte RAM, 75 MHz Pentium 540 Mbyte hard-disc
CD-ROM drive	Quad speed, CD-ROM XA, multi-session
Audio	16-bit sound card, wavetable MIDI, 3W per channel speakers
Graphics	Frame buffer direct access, resolution 352 x 240 at 30 frames per second
Video	Graphics facility with MPEG1 implemented in either hardware or software with support for video/audio stream (no frame dropping)

specifications for MPC2 and MPC3 are laid out in Tables 2 and 3 respectively. Realistically, only MPC3 should be considered since MPC2 also will soon be out of date.

When buying a multimedia PC you should ensure that it conforms to the MPC3 specifications, otherwise you will be disappointed with its performance especially when using it to play back PC video.

SOUND FEATURES

Music and sound are two of the vital ingredients of the multimedia concept which is experiencing successful commercial growth in the 1990s. To realise the opportunities of music and sound on a PC it is necessary to install a **sound card**. If you have a CD-ROM drive in your PC a sound card is a must since so many multimedia CD-ROMs require sound facilities. When you buy a multimedia PC it will probably have a sound card already installed in it. What you must check is that the quality of the sound it produces is acceptable. The sound card is accommodated in one of the expansion slots in the PC and is relatively easy to set up. Typically, a good quality sound card will be furnished with facilities for processing sound and for exercising control on electronic musical instruments via the **Music Instrument Digital Interface** (MIDI).

The sound card

Many sound cards are capable of reproducing high fidelity stereo sound normally associated with domestic compact disc units on a hi-fi (Digital Audio Tape – DAT). The sound card itself is capable of producing the audio signals only, and the signal must be fed into an amplifier system (a hi-fi unit, for example). The so-called **multimedia PCs** (MPCs) come with their own sound card, amplifier and loudspeaker units. The audio outputs from a sound card are standard RCA phono connectors (red and white – one for each channel), the same as are found on a domestic hi-fi amplifier, and it is therefore very easy to connect the two. Connecting the sound card to a hi-fi unit is preferable to using speakers supplied with the PC – the sound quality will be much better. The features on a sound card include the ability to:

- record and play back CD quality sound
- enhance recorded sounds by signal processing
- play audio CDs loaded in the CD-ROM drive
- play sound tracks from video files
- convert text into speech
- enable MIDI instruments to be interfaced to the PC.

There are many sound cards on the market and a typical example is the **Sound Blaster AWE64** from **Creative Labs** which is PnP compatible (see Chapter 2) and is capable of performing the above list of operations. We can now look further at the features in the above list and discuss how they can be accessed on the PC.

Processing and generating audio signals

There are several features on a sound card which are involved in the processing and generation of audio signals. A good quality sound card will have the standard 16-bit precision. The **Analogue to Digital Converter** (ADC) in the sound card slices up the input analogue signal into digital samples which are stored as numbers. The number of samples produced every second is known as the **sampling**

rate. For CD quality audio sound reproduction this needs to be 44,100 samples every second (44.1 kHz – frequency is measured in Hertz or Hz – events per second). Such a sound card is normally capable of receiving audio signals from at least three sources:

- a matched pair of stereo microphones
- an analogue input (radio or cassette – denoted **line in**)
- a CD-ROM drive in the PC.

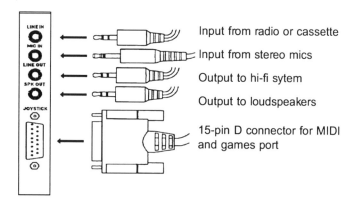

Fig. 7. Connections on a typical sound card.

The first two in this list are fed through 3 mm jacks on the rear of the sound card (see Figure 7). Audio speech can be recorded with a sound card and stored as digital data usually in .wav (wave) or .voc (vocoder) files. These can be played back as needed and can in fact be implanted in documents as sound icons. Sound files embedded in documents can also be sent as e-mail messages to remote PCs via your telephone line (see Chapter 6).

Memory storage for sound
The user will have control over the amount of memory occupied by the audio files by setting:

- the conversion rate (the rate at which the analogue signal is sampled)
- the precision (8-bit or 16-bit)
- whether to record in mono or stereo.

It should be kept in mind that stereo sound files with 16-bit precision take up a great deal of memory (10 seconds will take up 4 Mbyte). However, there are options for compressing sound files so they occupy less memory space (using .voc file format). These days, with large hard-disc capacities, it's quite straightforward to perform hard-disc recording – record music or speech directly onto the hard-disc. A one-minute CD quality stereo recording will need 10.6 Mbyte of hard-disc space. If you are interested in making your own audio CDs you will require:

- a CD-Recorder (see Chapter 5)
- sufficient hard-disc capacity to hold your audio music files to enable the CD to be made in one session.

However, you may have an application where you can afford to relax the sound quality conditions; for example if you are interested in making audio speech files for teaching or training purposes you could:

- reduce the sampling rate to 20 kHz
- record in mono
- use sound compression (.voc files).

You could therefore achieve a longer playing time for the same memory capacity. Information on how to do this can be found in the Windows help file on multimedia.

Synthesising the human voice
Many sound cards host a **Digital Signal Processor** (DSP) chip which is useful for the purposes of synthesising the human voice. It is very easy to configure the PC to act as a **Text to Speech** converter. There are a number of utilities for performing this task. For example, when **Texto'LE Annotation** (a **Sound Blaster** product) is invoked, you open the folder (or file) containing the text, then mouse click on the annotate icon and off it goes. The result is document reconstituted as speech – even if it does sound a little American! You do, however, have a number of voices to choose from and you also have the option to fashion a voice. The dictionary used by this feature can be augmented by using a phonetic spelling style.

Choosing sound software
Part of Windows are the multimedia drivers which are denoted as

the **Media Control Interface** (MCI). These are modified (if necessary) by accessing the drivers icon via the **Control Panel** option. A number of drivers can be installed from this dialogue box. Typical MCI drivers will include controllers for:

- **CD Audio**, for playing music CDs.

- **Sound**, for allowing the Microsoft record and playback facilities to be accessed. When the multimedia menu is invoked, the user has the option of choosing the sound recording facility which results in the feature shown in Figure 8. Overall, the number of options offered with this is somewhat limited and you would be better off using the software that comes with the accompanying sound card.

Fig. 8. The sound recorder in Windows.

- MIDI Sequencer, for enabling the MIDI option to become active.

These features can be accessed through the media player which is shown in Figure 9. As you can see, some of the control buttons resemble those found on a cassette recorder: play, pause, fast forward and rewind.

Fig. 9. The Windows media player.

Bundled software

When you buy a sound card you will invariably have bundled with it a suite of software which offers a range of facilities which are not too dissimilar to the features offered by the Windows MCI. For example, the **Sound Blaster** software offers a suite of software packages that among other things simulates a hi-fi system with sliders that are operated by the mouse action. You will also find other features corresponding to the typical controls found on a domestic hi-fi.

LOOKING AT THE CD-ROM DRIVE

It will come as no surprise to learn that a sound card is normally paired with a CD-ROM drive since they form part of the multimedia specification of an MPC. It is customary these days to have PCs that support EIDE (see Chapter 2) where the CD-ROM drive is connected directly to the motherboard. In previous designs (IDE) you had to install a ribbon cable between the sound card and the CD-ROM drive. Data from the CD-ROM therefore transferred to the PC system via the sound card.

Many multimedia CD-ROMs have audio files, which are played by the sound card while the image and text files are passed onto the CPU for processing. A CD-ROM drive will also play conventional CDs. There is a facility in Windows, CD Player (shown in Figure 10), which recognises when a music CD is in the drive and will play it when the PC is powered up.

Fig. 10. The CD player from Windows.

The CD-ROM standards – the Colour Books

The standards by which data are set out on a CD-ROM is published in a series of so-called **Colour Books**. When the CD first came onto the market it only contained audio files to be played on domestic CD players. As the CD evolved as a general purpose medium for storing not only audio files but also images, text, video and sound files, then the standards by which the data were stored on the CD needed to be revised and the standards are laid out in the various Colour Books. You will find that new multimedia equipment will conform to the most recent set of standards. Although as a user of CD-ROMs you will not have to concern yourself directly with these standards, they are often quoted in relation to the specification of CD-ROM drives.

Enhanced CDs

These are CDs that contain normal audio tracks and interactive material usually found on ordinary CD-ROMs. When inserted in a domestic hi-fi CD player only the audio tracks are played, whereas when an enhanced CD is placed in a PC's CD-ROM drive the whole disc can be accessed as a normal CD-ROM (including the audio tracks). The enhanced CD is an attractive medium for carrying pop music-video material and the music can be played simultaneously. These are becoming a very popular medium for marketing video footage.

MAKING MUSIC WITH MIDI

Another key aspect of the multimedia specification is MIDI (Musical Instrument Digital Interface), which is the standard method for controlling electronic musical instruments. By linking a PC to an instrument which has MIDI it's a simple process to get the PC to play the instrument. Music is stored in MIDI files on the PC's hard-disc. The MIDI files contain information relating to notes, their duration, tempo and type of musical sound, which is passed to the instrument. The MIDI input and output channels on a sound card are embedded in the externally accessed D connector. A special adapter cable is available which has a mating D-connector on one end and the standard DIN MIDI connectors on the other. There are a number of MIDI format standards with regard to expansion cards, notably the **Roland MPO-401, Sound Blaster** and **AdLib**. When specifying a sound card, ensure that it is compatible with at least the Sound Blaster and MPO-401 formats. The titles of

MIDI files on the PC always end with .mid and can be played with the Media Player.

Music synthesis on the sound card

Sound cards have the ability to produce musical sounds that conform to the MIDI standards. There is, however, quite a variation in quality between the two methods for producing musical sounds:

- **Wave Table**: where actual real instrument sounds are sampled and stored in memory (Read Only Memory – ROM). To produce a tune the sampled sound is played at different pitches. There is, however, a limit on how far you can stretch a sampled sound from its original pitch. The character of a note played in the bass of a piano is quite different from that of one played from the higher octaves. Good quality Wave Tables will therefore have sampled sounds from three or four actual pitches which are then stretched to produce the desired pitch. In general you will find that quality sound cards will have a lot of ROM dedicated to the Wave Table (at least 4 Mbyte).

- **Frequency Modulation (FM)**: using digital signal generators to synthesise artificial sounds. During the 1970s this was quite novel, but by today's standards the quality of the sounds produced is really quite thin and dreadful – one wonders why sound card manufacturers bother to incorporate this feature on their cards. Not a feature widely used by the discerning ear.

In Windows you have the option of playing MIDI files using Wave Tables, FM or an external MIDI instrument. You can access this feature via the control box and multimedia icon.

Sound daughter boards (SDBs)

A sound card not possessing a Wave Table can be modified by adding a daughter board (SDB) that hosts a Wave Table, thereby improving the sound quality. The majority of SDBs have a timbre of 16 instruments and a polyphony of 28 notes (see below). Digital acoustic effects such as reverberation and echoes can also be added onto the sounds. An SDB is attached directly to the sound card. The software provided with a number of SDBs will also allow you to modify the shape of the sound stored in ROM; for example, attack, sustain and decay. Typical SDBs are **Orchid WaveBooster** and the **Yamaha DB50XG**.

MIDI instruments

A MIDI instrument, such as a synthesiser or a sound module which conforms to the general MIDI standard, can simulate 128 instrumental sounds, although **Roland** have an extension of this standard called **GS**. There are two terms often used when specifying electronic musical instruments:

- **Timbre**, the number of instruments that can play at any one time. Normally 16 different instruments – one per MIDI channel.

- **Polyphony**, the number of simultaneous notes that each of the 16 instruments can play at the same time – normally 32 notes for modern sound cards.

The quality of sounds produced from an upmarket synthesiser far exceeds the sounds from a typical sound card. You would expect this since a quality keyboard will cost £1,000 + compared to £200 for a sound card. If you are interested in high quality sounds, forget about the sound card and concentrate on a MIDI instrument (synthesiser or workstation). There is a considerable number of MIDI synthesisers on the market and these days the range of sounds they can generate is quite extraordinary. Two such instruments are the **Quadraverb plus Piano** from **Alesis** and the **E96** from **Roland**.

A PC can play a synthesiser by feeding it with the data from a standard MIDI file (.mid). The information in the MIDI file contains all the data needed for controlling the performance from the synthesiser. These include:

- choice of instruments (timbre)
- polyphony (the number of notes)
- pitch
- volume
- length of notes
- velocity (how hard a key is pressed)
- after touch (note release)
- musical style (drum patterns)
- special effects such as:
  1. reverberation
  2. pitch bend
  3. stereo positioning
  4. chorus.

These are the standard features which are controlled by the PC. For complex synthesisers or sound modules (a MIDI instrument without a keyboard) there's likely to be a larger range of control options. However, to obtain effective control of a MIDI synthesiser you will require the appropriate music software and there are many packages on the market of varying quality. A list is included in Appendix A.

MIDI sequencing
The PC can also accept data from a MIDI instrument and this is essential for composition purposes. As the musician plays the instrument, the notes can be made to appear on the PC screen in proper musical notation and recorded. This real-time process of recording MIDI data is called **sequencing** and is regarded as a fundamental requirement of a PC-based MIDI system. There are many sequencing software packages on the market, but in general they form part of a suite of music facilities.

Sequencing software
This allows the user to record from the MIDI synthesiser one channel (a stave of music) at a time. As the channel is played back a second channel can be played by the musician which is recorded and overlays the first. The processes can be continued to produce a small-scale composition. A metronome is also provided to help synchronise the sequencing. In a recording studio you will always find a mixer – the large unit with hundreds of knobs and sliders on. Software mixers are also available and an example is shown in Figure 11 from the Musicator for Windows software. The sliders on the display control the volume of each channel and the user has the option of attaching any instrument to any channel.

Choosing music software
In order to realise the full potential of the PC for music application purposes it is necessary to have the appropriate software running on the PC. Although there is a reasonable amount of commercial software available it will be necessary for you to specify your requirements to avoid buying the wrong software. Most quality music software is in the price range £200 – £700. However, most music software runs under Windows and has the usual cut and paste features similar to those found in wordprocessors. Several music software products offer a range of facilities and these include the following:

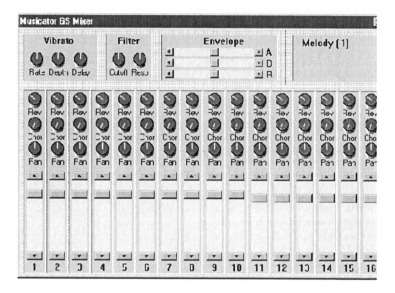

Fig. 11. A typical software mixing desk.

- **Notator**: this software utility allows you to produce a high quality notated music score. A quality notator will have all the editing features that you need to produce a conventional musical score. The pages of the score can be seen on the PC screen and the notator will produce a **what you see is what you get** (WYSIWYG) print out on a laser printer. In addition to the music you should also be able to place words, lyrics and their extensions anywhere on the score.

- **Sequencer**: a utility for recording musical notes from a MIDI keyboard and displaying them in a music notation form. As the music is played back additional parts can be added in real-time from the MIDI keyboard, so allowing the user to build up a score.

- **Score editing**: during composition, it is imperative for the user to edit their composition. The editing facilities should contain all the features which are normally available for generating proper musical scores.

- **General features**: in addition to the features listed above, a music software package should be able to:
  1. Perform transposition and effect key changes very easily.

2. Combine parts to generate a single score (and the reverse).
3. Generate separate staves from a stave containing chords.
4. Edit by using cut, copy and paste as in a wordprocessor.
5. Add sound effects and balancing using a screen-based mixer to control pan, chorus, reverberation and voice volume.
6. Create MIDI files (.mid) from scores.

These are the general features that you would expect, but most music software packages have their own unique features. Composition using a MIDI keyboard coupled to a PC has never been easier.

USING THE GAMES PORT

Most sound cards come with a games port embedded in the 15-pin D-connector on the back plane of the card. A joy stick or similar control column can be interfaced to the PC via the games port. A typical games joy stick will have four sensors for motion – forward, backward, left and right – and a variety of buttons.

However, more sophisticated joy sticks will have additional features. If you really want to make the most of your games it may well be worth considering a joy stick. If you are keen on flight simulators then a joy stick is a must. You will find several types of joy sticks in your local computer shop. In the Windows control panel you will find a joy stick icon which allows you to select the type or model of device that you are using. There is, however, not a lot else that you do with the games port apart from using it with games software.

PLAYING AND CREATING VIDEO

One area where multimedia development has been advancing is that of realising video on the PC. We will distinguish between two requirements: playing video files and creating video files on the PC. They are quite different and require different peripherals – the latter will require editing. Many feature films are now available on CD-ROM and can be played on a PC provided with appropriate video playback facilities (an interface card).

Video on Windows

VHS players and camcorders have been available for several years and it will come as no surprise to learn that it is relatively easy to interface one to a PC so that sequential images (a video file) can be stored. Within Windows is a feature called **Video for Windows**, which is a component of Microsoft's multimedia facility. It allows video files (.AVI) to be played back on the PC monitor. Before we progress any further we must take a closer look at the current standards used in PC video technology.

Display Control Interface (DCI)

Current PC graphics cards, often referred to as **graphics accelerator cards**, when used to show video material (also known as video footage) require the use of the **Display Control Interface** (DCI). This is a software utility that enables Windows to exploit the full features of the graphics for reproducing video material. All quality graphics cards should support the DCI and when specifying a graphics card make sure that it's DCI compliant otherwise the quality of the video playback is likely to be poor.

Compressing information

When dealing with video information (moving images) large amounts of memory and fast data throughputs are required. A single frame from a VCR stored on a VHS tape requires 1.3 Mbyte of storage data and the throughput is 25 per second. For just one second of viewing you would require 33 Mbyte of data storage on your hard-disc. Fortunately a number of clever techniques have been developed to enable image information to be compressed thereby relaxing the need for large storage capacity.

A compression algorithm known as **M-JPEG** (Motion - Joint Photographers Expert Group) has been adopted and relies on storing the difference between image frames. This works on the principle that there's no point in storing information that doesn't change from frame to frame. In reality one frame in every 15 is stored complete and only the differences in the successive 14 are stored (referred to as P-frames). From the P-frames a near true image can be restored.

Video footage in M-JPEG format is relatively easy to edit owing to its random access (any frame can accessed easily). You will find that a number of software packages will perform this task.

MPEG

To achieve better digital video compression an alternative algorithm has been devised and this has been adopted by the **Motion Picture Expert Group** (MPEG). Levels of compression using MPEG can exceed 50:1 thereby saving a lot of disc space. For example, a 74-minute VHS video (with audio) can be stored onto a 650 Mbyte CD-ROM. There are in fact two standards: MPEG, which relates to the CD-ROM with a data transfer rate of 1.2 Mbits/s; and MPEG-2 which specifies a data transfer rate of between 5 and 10 Mbits/s and is applicable to high resolution video satellite TV decoders. The latter standard is currently used in upmarket professional products for producing air time quality transmissions (Digital Betacam). It will soon become the standard for home video editing and processing. This will involve the use of the new digital VHS tapes from JVC and Panasonic.

Video play-back

Having considered the standards used in PC video technology we can now move on to consider video playback since many CD-ROMs are available with feature films on. A simple video file (.AVI – audio video interlace) can be played using the Video for Windows or QuickTime software. However, if you require your PC to play CD-ROM video you will require a utility that supports MPEG. This is achieved by using either a software package or a hardware graphics processor on the graphics card.

Software MPEG player

The well-known MPEG software player is **Xing** from Xing Technology although it should be mentioned that to achieve a reasonable display you will require a high performance PC – at least a Pentium running at 90 MHz. MPEG software does put considerable strain on the CPU and the overall performance will be poor compared with using a hardware solution.

Hardware MPEG player

You will not be surprised to learn that a hardware MPEG player comes in the form of a PC expansion card which can be inserted into your PC. The MPEG standard specifies an image size of 352 x 288 pixels (picture elements). However, this is normally doubled up, although even so it will not occupy the whole of the PC screen. MPEG player cards have a dedicated processor for performing the MPEG decoding thereby reducing the load on the CPU. There are two common designs for implementing MPEG in hardware:

- MPEG card working in parallel with your current graphics card
- all-in-one graphics and MPEG card(s).

In the first design, the MPEG image is overlaid onto the image from the graphics card image. In effect the MPEG replaces part of the graphics card image. This is achieved by having an external loop-back cable carrying the SVGA signals from the graphics card to the MPEG card. The monitor lead is then connected to the MPEG card. An example of such a card is the **REALmagic LITE** from **Sigma Designs**.

The alternative design encompasses the MPEG and the normal graphics hardware on a single graphics card. As the MPEG requirement becomes more widespread this design will become more commonplace. An example of such a graphics card is the **ShowTime Plus** from **SPEA**.

Creating video footage with a PC

Equipment is on the market for creating professional quality video tape footage that's suitable for television broadcast. These are up-market products costing from £5,000 upwards and are beyond the scope of this book. There are, however, more economical products aimed at the domestic market for creating home video footage. You will need a minimum of a 100 MHz Pentium-based PC, at least 16 Mbyte of RAM and free hard-disc space of 2.2 Gbyte – preferably SCSI-2 (see Chapter 2).

Image data can be obtained from a VCR or a camcorder. To transfer image data from either of these sources you will require a video image capture expansion card (or video capture card). These fall into two price categories. In the lower price range you will find video cards with ISA buses. For example, the Fast FPS 60 is an M-JPEG card which can be augmented with a daughter board to provide MPEG processing. This card can be used for capture and play-back.

At the higher end of the medium price market is the **Miro DC20** video card with a PCI bus and an SCSI adapter. The DC20 is a Plug and Play card and comes with **Vidcap32**, Microsoft's 32-bit video capture software. The connectors on the rear of the card include S-video in and S-video out and also composite video. You can therefore preview your recordings and edited footage. It requires an SCSI hard-disc (EIDE is not really up to the job because of its high CPU reliance). The DC20 is appropriate for producing multimedia video footage (.AVI files) with a compression ratio of 5:1. This card produces Betacam quality (comparable with broadcast video) footage and will definitely appeal to the semi-professional user.

Video editing software

Fortunately when you buy a video card you will normally get some video editing software bundled with the product. One of the well-known packages is **Premiere** from **Adobe** (Tel: (0131) 453 2211). Premiere is a very powerful package and allows a whole range of options for the user. Its design philosophy is similar to that of a wordprocessor. In effect you can treat video footage like you would treat a sentence in a wordprocessor – cut, paste, copy, insert and delete. You can even layer footage, fade, and add audio sound tracks with or without sound effects. Apart from the normal editing features you can also implement warping and a whole spectrum of distortion effects.

Other video editing software includes **Wave for Windows** from Turtle Beach. Needless to say, all this will only be useful provided you have quality video footage to begin with. You will therefore have to budget the whole system very carefully – don't forget the cost of a quality camcorder.

VIDEO CONFERENCING

It is a relatively straightforward task to implement a video conferencing system on a PC. Simultaneous visual and audio communication has a lot of appeal to it. Seeing as well as speaking to a person remotely has many advantages especially when there is a need to exchange live visual information. However, the technology is relatively young and as yet quite expensive for a truly practicable system.

From a video conferencing point-to-point link you will be able to:

- have audio speech communication
- have real-time vision of remote party
- share a white-board for exchanging ideas
- down-load data files from remote party.

However, the quality of the visual aspect of video conferencing is nothing to write home about. This will depend on the type of telephone line you are using. If you have an ISDN-2 link (see Chapter 5) to your PC the quality of the video will be quite acceptable.

If, on the other hand, you are using an ordinary telephone link (**Public Switched Telephone Network** (PSTN)) the visual quality will be pretty poor and the video area on the monitor will be only slightly larger than a Christmas postage stamp. The **bandwidth**, which is a measure of the information-carrying capacity of the PSTN, is very narrow as it was never intended to carry images.

Generally speaking, if you do not have access to an ISDN-2 your return on the capital outlay (£1,000 +) for a video conferencing system will be marginal. Since relatively few people have video conferencing hardware in their PC you should first establish a strong need before you go ahead and buy a video conferencing system.

As with all other multimedia PC technology there are standards that vendors have to conform to. These ensure that one manufacturer's video conferencing will work with others'.

Video conferencing standards

The first standard to consider in the field of video conferencing is the ITU-T H.320 recommendation. H.320 ensures that equipment made by different manufacturers is compatible. Point-to-point video conferencing has been extended to encompass **multipoint** conferencing – several users participating simultaneously in a conference. The standards for multipoint conferencing are known as the T.120 series. These are concerned with the overall management of multipoint conferencing. When buying video conferencing equipment ensure that it conforms to both H.320 and T.120 series specifications.

Video conferencing hardware

To enable video conferencing with your PC you will require a number of hardware features. These normally consist of:

- a small video camera with suitable mounting fixtures
- an expansion card to interface to the video camera
- a microphone and head set
- if you have an ISDN-2 link you will probably need a second card working in parallel with the first.

You will find that a commercial video conferencing package will have all these as standard items. The video camera is normally mounted on the PC's monitor and should not appear as an obtrusive fixture – hence the small size.

Video conferencing software

When you buy a video conferencing system for your PC it will include the necessary software to enable audio and video conferencing to take place. The software should also perform the following tasks:

- generate a video area on the monitor
- enable a bidirectional audio channel to be established
- have a directory of video conference users with instant dial up
- allow a common white-board to be constructed on the monitor so that your mouse and other party's mice can draw on it
- enable easy transfer of files from folders or directories.

An example of a video conferencing system that does not use ISDN is the **ShareVision PC3000** from **Creative Labs** – this is a total package including a modem (see Chapter 5). An example of a system that uses the ISDN link is the **ProShare Video System 200** from **Intel**. Both products come with two expansion cards each.

CHECKLIST

- Before you buy a multimedia PC to be used in a work environment, make sure that the sounds it's likely to produce will not interfere with other people. You may have to use headphones. Even these may be a nuisance.

- If you are buying a multimedia PC for CD-ROM video playback, ensure that there are sufficient titles on CD-ROMs in the subject area of interest. Ask in your local video tape shop.

- When using a PC linked to a MIDI keyboard, you may find it worthwhile loading up demo versions of music software. Make enquiries about the availability of this software by reading through one of the many music technology magazines such as *Sound on Sound* or *The Mix*.

CASE STUDIES

Having read through this chapter you will have realised that the scope for a multimedia PC is very broad. Several options have been considered showing how a PC may be modified to enhance its versatility and range of applications.

George requires a PC for composing and editing music

This is a very popular application for the PC. Many music students and composers use a PC for this purpose. George wants to play a MIDI keyboard and see the notes appear on the PC screen (sequencing). He will also want the music played back on the MIDI keyboard. Typically, George's hardware specifications will be:

- Multimedia PC with sound card and CD-ROM.

- External MIDI keyboard (synthesiser or workstation) with integral Wave Table sound facilities (prices start from £500).

- MIDI interface cable for connecting sound card to the MIDI instrument.

- Sound system (hi-fi) connected to the Line Out of the sound card. The connecting cable, with a red and white phono plug on one end and a 3 mm stereo jack plug on the other, is usually supplied with the sound card.

Having sorted out the hardware requirements, George needs to specify his music software. The minimum needs for the software are:

- Sequencing – take in notes from the MIDI keyboard either note by note or in real-time playing.

- Notate – produce a score.

- Allow editing of score.

- Enable multitrack sequencing – building tracks upon tracks in real-time.

- To generate MIDI files from the sequenced music.

There are numerous music software packages on the market and several perform all these functions (see Appendix A). There is, however, a variation in prices and in general the more you pay the more facilities you have.

Paul wants to create videos and market them on CD-ROM and VHS tapes

This is becoming a very popular application of the PC. Editing home video material is now both relatively easy and affordable.

Typically Paul will need a high performance PC with the following hardware and software specifications:

- A MMX-based PC (minimum 166 MHz) with:
  1. 32 Mbyte RAM
  2. 2 Gbyte SCSI-2 hard-disc
  3. SCSI-2 Interface card
  4. Graphics card with 4 Mbyte VRAM.

- A video capture card (a Miro DC20, for example).

- An MPEG video playback, such as REALmagic LITE.

- A Super-VHS video cassette recorder (VCR).

- A camcorder with composite outputs.

- A CD-R for making the CD-ROM (see Chapter 5).

- Software to perform the editing – when you buy a video capture card for the PC you will have software bundled for performing this task. You may also require additional software such as Premiere from Adobe.

- Software for preparing the video footage for downloading onto the CD-R. Again when you buy a CD-R you will probably have bundled software to perform this task.

After reading through the sales literature Paul will realise that the video capture expansion card will accept composite video signals from the camcorder and he can store these as M-JPEG files which permits easy editing. There will also be two outputs on the video card, to allow him to play the video files on his television and to store the finished product on an S-VHS tape-connection to the VCR. Paul will also be able to download his video footage as either an .AVI file or an MPEG file onto CD-ROM using the CD-R drive.

Martin's dad is going to buy him a PC for his 15th birthday
Although Martin has told his dad that he wants it to help him with the course work for his GCSEs he really wants it for playing games. Martin has to specify what PC configuration he wants. Games need fast graphics and good quality sounds. Typically Martin will need:

- MMX PC
- 32 Mbyte of RAM
- 2 Gbyte EIDE hard-disc
- 14inch SVGA colour monitor
- 64-bit graphics accelerator card
- sound card with Wave Table sounds
- joy stick (see Chapter 5)
- loudspeakers for sound reproduction
- CD-ROM drive for playing games CD-ROMs.

DISCUSSION POINTS

1. List the types of CD-ROM material that you or your family may be interested in and make enquiries in your local bookshops or computer store to see if they carry any stock that is relevant to your needs.

2. Do you think that a multimedia PC system will help productivity in your workplace and would it be financially viable to incur the additional costs?

3. Do you think that multimedia could be used as a training aid in your profession?

4. If the answer to the last question is yes, you may care to give some thought as to how this may be achieved.

5. Do you think that a video conferencing system will benefit your company now or in the future?

4
Buying PC Software

A PC without decent software is of limited use and when specifying a task for your PC don't forget to include in your overall budget the cost of the software. This chapter describes a selected range of software packages that are likely to appeal to the general user of a PC who has a need to process, collate and present information. It is important to remember that a great number of commercial software packages are very comprehensive in their design and options. This can be somewhat forbidding when you first start using it. However, you do not have to learn everything about it overnight – it may take several weeks, depending on your needs. It is worth remembering that it's probably taken hundreds of man-hours to create the product in the first place. You are therefore not going to, nor will you be expected to, master the ins and outs of a software package within a few hours.

USING PC SOFTWARE

It is unlikely that you will require all the facilities offered by most software that you choose to use. You should, however, be aware of what it's capable of doing and this information can usually be gleaned from the tutorial which accompanies most packages. You should therefore try and access the services that you require from the software. Try and focus your attention on those aspects which are going to serve your immediate needs – this way you can gain a working experience with the product.

Using software legally
One frequent failing when costing a new PC system is to inadequately budget for new software. Not only is it sound practice to use legal software (to become the registered user) but you also gain from the advantages of being a legitimate user. These include:

- Having a **User's Manual** and a **Reference Manual** – for a complex product these are essential.

- You can update the software at a special upgrade price.

- When you experience difficulties you will be able to contact the suppliers direct and discuss your problem with their technical department – known as technical support.

- You may, at some stage, wish to publish material that may necessitate the disclosure of using commercial software. If you are not a registered user or do not possess a legitimate copy of it the **Federation Against Software Theft** (FAST) will have an easy time convicting you.

Keeping up-to-date with software

There is a vast number of software packages on the market and the task of trying to determine what is the most suitable product for your intended purpose will not be easy. Table 1 in Chapter 1 lists several applications where the PC could play a role. The effectiveness of each application is realised through an appropriate software package. Consult the reference manual from **Chest** (see Appendix A) if you require a complete up-to-date listing of current software. In this chapter the commonly generic software will be discussed. These days such software is usually bundled with a new PC and serves as an extra carrot to attract new buyers.

UNDERSTANDING THE OPERATING SYSTEM

In order for a PC to work properly it has to have an operational environment, equivalent to a software framework in which programs can run with a minimum risk of failing. You can think of an operating system as a management regime with a set of rules to which the running program must conform. Sometimes these rules are violated and one of the functions of the management system is to mount a rescue mission to prevent the whole PC from coming to a total standstill (commonly known as a hang-up). Advanced operating systems allow several programs to run at the same time and Windows is an example. The operating system also facilitates the transfer of data from one program to another – this is known as **dynamic linking**. There are a number of operating systems on the market and the most popular, owing to successful pricing policy, come from the American company Microsoft.

Microsoft Windows is basically a **multitasking** management environment which allows you to run several programs and access system facilities in a very smooth and easy manner.

Much of today's proprietary software has been written to run under Windows. When buying a PC from new you are likely to find a version of Windows already loaded. If you do not already have Windows on your PC then you are strongly advised to acquire a copy.

Multitasking

One of the key features of Windows is the ability to have several programs active on the monitor at the same time. Referred to as **multitasking**, this enables the user to switch their attention from one application to another very easily. By using the **Windows Clip Board** facility, information can be carried from one application to another. This is only one way of transferring information from one program to another.

Graphics User Interface (GUI)

In order to set a standard for the appearance of software on the screen Microsoft were instrumental in establishing the **Graphics User Interface** (GUI – pronounced gooee). All software running under Windows therefore looks the same because of the conformity to GUI standards. The point and click action on menus using the mouse is part of GUI. Point and drag is also part of the GUI format. These are standard features of the GUI environment and all Windows software has adopted them.

Memory consumption

One of the problems of Windows is the large amount of hard-disc space it consumes. As each new application is added, it too will add features such as **dynamic linked libraries** (DLLs) to the Windows directories. If you remove the software from your system, DLLs invariably get left behind and in no time at all you have accumulated far too many superfluous files in the Windows directories. This is a fact of life. This is the danger of installing demo versions of software packages.

Once you have finished with it, you can rarely remove all of the bits and pieces that were installed with it, although there are some software packages that can identify these and remove them for you. The moral is, don't install demo versions of software unless you really need to. Although with today's hard-discs having memory capacities of hundreds of Mbyte this should not pose too much of a problem, nevertheless you should be aware of the risks.

MS-DOS

The **Disc Operating System** from Microsoft, which is normally called MS-DOS or just DOS, was the first operating system used on PCs. It takes care of the low-level transfer of information between the CPU and the peripherals such as the screen, the keyboard and the printer. MS-DOS is not needed for Windows, although if a PC has Windows it can be powered up into MS-DOS if required.

There is still a lot of good quality software around which runs under DOS. The same software can still run under Windows. When invoked under Windows an MS-DOS window will be generated and the program will run in the window. When running in a window it's likely to execute much slower than under MS-DOS alone owing to the fact that Windows can still run other programs at the same time. However, most of the current software is written for Windows, resulting in a decreasing need for DOS in the future.

Other management software

Windows is not the only multitasking management software available, but it is by far the most successful in terms of sales. Others are:

- **OS/2 Warp** from IBM. This was introduced to rival Windows and has many admirable features, but has not gained the expected success. When OS/2 is loaded onto your hard-disc it displaces MS-DOS which may be a disadvantage for some applications. However, there are facilities within OS/2 to allow many MS-DOS programs to execute. There are relatively few commercial software packages which have been written to run specifically under OS/2.

- **Windows NT** from Microsoft (**New Technology**), an expensive version of Windows which uses the full 32-bit capacity of the 486 and Pentium CPUs.

Microsoft Windows

The emphasis in this chapter will be on software that runs under Windows. The primary reason for this is the widespread adoption of Windows above the others cited above. The vast majority of PC software produced today is being written to run under Windows.

As the most popular operating system for the PC, Windows has a great deal to commend it. When you buy a new PC ensure that it comes preloaded with Windows. You should also ensure that you are provided with a CD-ROM version of Windows. When the famous start button is pressed on Windows,

the main menu emerges to offer you a path to the facilities on your PC. By moving the cursor up to Programs, a menu appears containing all the program folders on the hard-disc(s). However, shortcut icons can be created and placed anywhere on the background screen. A double click with the mouse on an application program icon launches you into the program. At the top right corner of each program there are three buttons:

The button on the left causes the program to minimise to an icon on the Task bar at the bottom of the screen. By clicking on the icon the program is restored. It is therefore very easy to have several programs active at the same time and pass between them. The centre button causes the program to occupy the whole screen or just a window on the screen, whereas the button on the right closes the program completely. All Windows programs will have the three button feature in the top right corner of the application and several programs can run at the same time.

Multiple programs
Windows is known as a **multiprocessing operating system** which means that several programs can appear to run simultaneously. Each running program occupies its own window. The advantage of

this scheme is that it allows you to transfer information (data) easily from one program to another. Each program runs independently of all the others and part of Windows is to provide a protection scheme. If one program crashes (goes wrong – these things happen all too often) then it happens in isolation. It should not affect other programs running at the same time. Although you will probably lose data in the crashed program, all the others should remain intact. Each running program has an icon positioned at the base of the screen (**task bar**). By clicking on the icon the task becomes the foreground window. To help you familiarise yourself with Windows, Microsoft has provided a tutorial.

Windows tutorial
When you first power up your new PC with Windows you can run the tutorial and this will give you a guided tour of the product. It is a worthwhile exercise as it will give you a working knowledge and, more importantly, the confidence of using it. The tutorial can be accessed from the Windows Installation CD-ROM that will come with your new PC and it will show you how to create files.

Plug and Play
One of the attractive aspects of Windows is the Plug and Play (PnP) feature. This relates to the operation of the expansion cards inserted into the PC. Before Windows it was necessary to ensure that there were no conflicts between cards. These would normally come in three flavours, Input/Output address (I/O), Interrupts (INT) and Direct Memory Access channels (DMA). Sometimes these led to great difficulties especially among new users of PCs. To some extent PnP resolves all types of conflicts. However, it's by no means without problems. Ideally with PnP you require:

- PnP BIOS extension on the motherboard (see Chapter 2). You will see the PnP banner on the screen when you power up your PC. Your new PC should have a PnP BIOS.

- PnP compatible expansion cards. Try and specify this when buying a new expansion card.

In principle all you have to do now is insert the new expansion card into the PC and Windows will reconfigure itself to accommodate the new card. Windows running on a PC with a PnP BIOS will make an attempt to resolve conflict problems even with a non PnP expansion

card. If a conflict does arise Windows will notify you of the problem
and you will have to solve the problem manually.

Control Panel
Once you get into Windows one of the useful features for analysing
the hardware and software resources of the PC is the **Control Panel**.
When it is evoked it looks a bit like Figure 12. If you want to correct
the time, adjust the speed of the mouse, or alter the background
pattern on the monitor, evoke the Control Panel. Once you click on
an icon a set of dialogue boxes appears that enables you to make
your modification. If you are uncertain there is a help option which
gives information on each option offered to you. Although it takes a
little practice to begin with you will soon get used to it and feel quite
confident about using it.

Fig. 12. The Control Panel in Windows allows you easily to
make changes to the operation of your PC.

Wizards
One of the innovations of Windows is the use of Wizards. When you
install a new software application on a PC that has been designed to
run under Windows, you will be presented with a sequence of

dialogue boxes that offers you choices. These are referred to as Wizards and are designed to help you install or update software on your PC. They will lead you through a series of options until you have successfully completed the software installation. If you encounter a feature that you don't understand you can evoke a help facility that explains the significance of the feature.

Internet connection

One principal difference between Windows 98 and its predecessor is the high level of connectivity to the Internet (see Chapter 6). In fact a number of Internet tools form part of the Windows 98 operating system; as soon as it starts up, users can choose Active Desktop. This is somewhat similar to the Explorer Web Browser (see Chapter 6) and allows users to browse system resources as if they are web features. In effect the Active Desktop enables access to the Internet as if it's part of the user interface. In the same way as you have short cut icons to programs, Windows 98 has short cut icons to web addresses. You will also find NetShow for broadcasting information over the Internet and NetMeeting that enables collaborative communications which are similar to video conferencing features (see Chapter 3). To enable a fast rate of communication Windows 98 supports 56 kbs modems (see Chapter 5) and also has an ISDN Wizard to set up multiple modems.

WHAT TO LOOK FOR IN A WORDPROCESSOR

It is highly likely that if you are going to become a PC owner or user then you will need the services of a wordprocessor, for example, editing with undo, cut, copy, paste, delete, to name just a few functions. Current wordprocessors can do far more than their predecessors of even five years ago. Many now offer the type of control options at one time only found on **Desktop Publishing** (DTP) packages; for example creating maths equations, tables, graphs and image manipulation. Although you may not require all the options on offer, you should be aware of them in case you need them at a later time.

When you install the software there will be a tutorial that offers you a promenade introduction to its options. There are several wordprocessors which run under Windows; for example Microsoft Word, WordPerfect and Word Pro. Many features are common to all so it's only necessary to consider one in any great detail – namely Word Pro.

Looking closer at Word Pro

One of the front runners in the word processing market is **Word Pro** from **Lotus** which forms part of the Lotus integrated software package **SmartSuite**. The front end display of Word Pro is built upon Microsoft's **Graphics User Interface** (GUI) and all its functions can be accessed either from drop-down menu options or through an extensive array of SmartIcons which is a speciality of Word Pro. In fact, Word Pro has a very large number of SmartIcons, a selection of which can be displayed on the screen as and when they are required. The new user therefore has the opportunity to choose which SmartIcons they want displayed, which will depend on the range of services that are frequently accessed. Since Word Pro conforms to the GUI design, the user has a large choice of fonts to work with. Whatever fonts are available in the Windows directory can be used within a Word Pro document.

Word Pro Features

Word Pro is first and foremost a wordprocessing (WP) package and it comes with a rich selection of tools which you would expect from a modern WP package. The **editing** facilities consist of the usual features with many extras such as drag and drop. This enables a highlighted segment of text to be moved from one part of a document to another by simply clicking the mouse on the segment and moving the mouse to the new position. Alternatively, the scissors SmartIcon can be used.

With the option of having several documents open at any one time, it is very easy to copy or move text from one to another by using the Windows **ClipBoard** facility. It is also very easy to import text which may be in the format of other wordprocessors. Word Pro will convert them while still retaining the original style.

The user has considerable control over the **layout** of the pages (number of columns), the indentation of the paragraphs, footers and headers. For large documents it may be necessary to produce a table of contents and an index and Word Pro has facilities for creating these with relative ease.

As with other wordprocessing packages, Word Pro has the customary **spell checker** and **thesaurus**. It also has a **grammar checker**: not only the writing style can be checked but also a range of grammatical errors.

Having discussed very briefly the general wordprocessing features of Word Pro we can go on to examine the more advanced aspects which are characteristic of modern WP software.

Generating tables

A requirement which often arises is to show information in a tabular format. Tables consist of rows and columns which give rise to **cells.** When creating a table in Word Pro the user has considerable choice in the layout of the table. Not only the positioning of the table but also the size of the rows and columns, their shading (colour if needed) and the positioning of the lines around and in the table. Once a table has been created the user can enter into each cell, text, numerical data, an equation, an image, a drawing or a chart. The cell items can be edited in a similar fashion to text outside the table. It is also possible to Paste Link data from another package (such as Lotus 1-2-3) which supports **dynamic linked libraries** (DLLs) or **dynamic data exchange** (DDE). As with a normal spreadsheet you can perform calculations on specified cells (or arrays of cells) of numerical data. The syntax is the same as that found in the famous spreadsheet software package Lotus 1-2-3.

Generating charts

Word Pro has the provision for generating a variety of charts. Charts are useful for showing cursory trends in data movement and for data comparisons. The array of possible designs is somewhat limited compared with the options offered by **Stanford Graphics**, for example. However, the range, including column, bar, pie and area charts, is quite adequate for illustrating relatively small data sets which you may require to be displayed graphically. The data for each chart can be entered manually from the keyboard or fetched from the ClipBoard which must have previously been loaded with data. The data should have a form similar to that of a table with rows and columns. If the data input is changed for any reason, then by redrawing the chart the new information will enter the display. The user has the choice of colour selection including a reasonable range of greys which are needed for printing on a laser printer.

Drawing diagrams

An essential aspect of any wordprocessing package these days is the ability to import or create diagrams. All diagrams which are created or imported into Word Pro are positioned in frames. The frames may have text flowing around them or stand alone. When the Draw Mode is invoked an array of SmartIcons appears at the top of the screen. These represent all the objects that can be used to create diagrams: these consist of line styles, fill patterns, polygons, arcs, text and several others. For coarse drawing, the lines snap to grid points. For a more detailed drawing the snap option can be disabled, although the lines are a little more difficult to control. A drawing will therefore consist of an array of objects which can be edited individually. However, in contrast to specialised drawing software, the drawing features in Word Pro are intended only for small-scale drawings.

Importing images

Word Pro also allows the user to import images into a document. After a frame has been created an image can be imported into the frame. One of the very confusing aspects of PC software is the enormous range of **image file formats**. These formats relate to the way images and pictures are stored in memory. There are at least a dozen of them which have grown up over the years. One well-known example is the **tagged image file** (.tif) format. Fortunately various image file formats are recognised by Word Pro which makes this task quite simple. For example, the image may be imported from a flatbed scanner. Once an image has been positioned in a frame the user has a number of options for modifying it. It's even possible to perform some rudimentary image processing on the picture. These include brightness, contrast, smoothing and edge enhancement.

Images and memory

To improve the printing quality, the user also has the option of introducing halftones in the grey scales. There is, however, one major penalty of importing images into a document and that is memory – images will take up a great deal of memory. If you are intending to use many images in your documents then you are strongly advised to have a hard-disc with a storage capacity of at least 500 Mbyte.

USING SPREADSHEETS

The spreadsheet software within the **Lotus SmartSuite** is **Lotus 1-2-3** and has been the market leader for over ten years. When there is a requirement to store, manipulate and process numerical data a spreadsheet is probably one of the best options to use. A spreadsheet is structured as an array of cells and data are entered into each cell. Cells can be collected into columns, rows or both to generate an array.

Processing rows and columns

Processing can be performed on an individual column, or row, or an array. For example, by entering into a column the weekly spending, the cell directly under the column can be a calculation of the sum of the column cells. If you change the contents of one of the cells the sum cell is recalculated automatically. You can also enter comments into cells to allow description entry to be included in the spreadsheets. Most Windows spreadsheets have an impressive array of mathematical and statistical operations which can be applied to columns or rows of data. For example, given a column of figures, you can define a set of cells to hold the statistics relating to the column, mean, standard deviation, maximum and so forth.

Generating graphs

Having generated rows or columns of numbers you may wish to show the information graphically. This is easily done within a spreadsheet. One column can represent the x-axis and another column the y-axis of your graph. The graph can be generated by entering menu and working through or by using the graph icon.

Business Plan

If you are thinking of approaching a money lender, a bank for instance, for finance to support a new enterprise you will require a business plan. Fundamental to the business plan is the spreadsheet which should clearly demonstrate that you know what you are talking about and have a realistic plan for the intended enterprise. There are, however, software packages designed specifically for this purpose and an example is **Business Plan** from **PlanIT** (see Appendix A).

USING DATABASES

When applications arise where lots of information needs to be processed, whether image, text, sound file or whatever, a database is a suitable environment to perform this task. Databases broadly come in two varieties, flatfile and relational.

Flatfile databases

A flatfile database is somewhat similar to a card index box where the records of information completely stand alone. It is almost impossible to perform any cross-referencing between data records in a flatfile database. You do, however, have options to search for words (strings) and the database should display the records that have common words within their titles or embedded in their text. A popular database that offers more than just a flatfile design is **File Maker Pro** from **Claris**.

Relational databases

The majority of databases are of this design and are in general more useful and flexible. In essence a relational database has its data distributed over several table sets which are closely integrated. Each table is able to serve a different purpose. Making a modification in one table will automatically ripple through the table set. As an illustration consider the example in Figure 13. Three divisions within the same company require different uses of the stored data relating to their customers. The database as seen by each department appears quite different – reflecting the needs of the department. By storing the information in a relational database the data become common to each department although the needs are different.

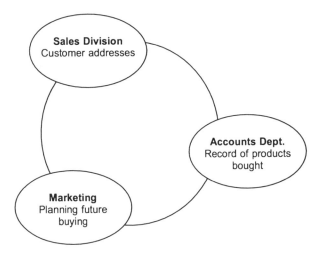

Fig. 13. Database information access by different departments.

Searches and queries

One of the principal requirements of a database is the ability to set up a search query to distil the information into a well-defined table. For example, given a database of customers you could generate a table of customers in the Brighton area who gave custom of over

£3,000 between May and October of last year. This is an easy task for a database search to perform. Most database software will allow you to construct a query operation, probably through a series of dialogue boxes where you enter your search criterion involving and/or decisions.

Once the search is complete you could have a table containing the names and addresses of the customers, the products they bought and even details of when their account was settled. The amount of detail you have in the resulting table depends on how much you request from the query operation.

WHAT'S IN AN INTEGRATED OFFICE SUITE?

These days it is customary when buying a new PC to have bundled with it an array of software that will appeal to the general user. Quite often this software will include an **Integrated Office Suite** (IOS). A typical IOS will comprise:

- a wordprocessor
- a spreadsheet
- a database
- an office planner
- a scheduler
- graphics presentation software.

There are several IOSs on the market and four well-known ones are:

- **Works 95** from **Microsoft** (runs under Windows)
- **Office 97** from **Microsoft** (runs under Windows)
- **SmartSuite** from **Lotus**
- **PerfectOffice** from **Novell**.

One of the key features of the individual members of each IOS is the ability to link and exchange information with the other packages in the IOS. As an example of this operation consider the graphics presentation software and the spreadsheet. Each time a change is made in the spreadsheet the graphs in the presentation software change automatically. This is achieved by means of the **Object Linked and Embedding protocol** (OLE). OLE is a so-called object interface that allows objects (groups of data) to transfer from one application to another. An important part of this scheme is the mutual recognition of data by disparate software packages.

Bundled software

Some suppliers of PCs will include an IOS with some of their PC models as bundled software. It is certainly worth considering. To get an idea of what to expect from each component of an IOS let's consider one in a little more detail. For this purpose we shall look at Microsoft's **Office 97** designed for Windows.

USING OFFICE 97

As an example of an IOS, Office 97 contains a whole range of utilities and applications that one would find useful in an office environment. Written to run under Windows, it has not only the usual features expected from an IOS for an office environment but also a number of additional ones.

When using Office 97 you are encouraged to think of your requirements first and not the program software. Hence the icons ask you to open a document or create a new one without any reference as to whether it's a spreadsheet, wordprocessor or database. With the emphasis on integration, the boundary between these tasks becomes quite artificial. Once Office 97 has been installed on your PC several icons become resident on the screen and these help you to perform one of the following:

- open a document
- create a new document
- make an appointment.

Office binder

An interesting feature of Office 97 is the Office Binder, which allows you to collect together all the information relating to a project into one folder. Whether spreadsheets, text documents or databases, they can be collected to form a binder with a consistent appearance and with sequential page numbers. By collating information into a single binder the process of printing is much simplified to produce a uniform looking document even though the information is from different sources.

Wizards

To help you gain confidence in each application in Office 97 extensive use is made of Wizards (see above). With the Wizards you can ask questions such as 'How do I ...'. In return you will get dialogue boxes showing you step-by-step answers to enable you to achieve your objective.

Using Word

The wordprocessor within Office 97 is an updated version of Microsoft's **Word for Windows** and contains all the features that one would expect from a quality wordprocessor. The spell check works in real-time (the words are checked as you type them) – if you spell a word incorrectly it is highlighted with a red line. A greater emphasis has been placed on the importance of templates. There is a large variety to choose from and they are organised into various groups; for example, letters, memoranda, faxes, document headings and layouts. You have what are known as placeholders to assist you to position information in the appropriate positions in documents. Provided your PC is linked up to a network (see Chapter 7) it is very easy to use Word as an email editor to highlight text and send it to another user on the network.

Using Excel

This is a comprehensive spreadsheet program that has evolved through many iterations. All the features described in the spreadsheet section above are included in Excel. Several spread-sheets can be active at the same time and Excel allows you to transfer information from one to another using the mouse assisted drag and drop method. You can also transfer information between Excel and other Office 97 programs, Access for example. There is, however, an interesting feature for displaying data visually, not only as graphs but also as maps. If you have tabular information relating to geographical data, the information can be relayed directly onto maps. A Data Map icon enables you to generate from tables coloured regions of areas or countries as the case may be.

Preparing presentations

Today it is commonplace for marketing purposes to use the PC as a presentation platform and **PowerPoint** is well suited to this task. In effect if you want to make a presentation with slides, text, images, animation footage and sound files, then PowerPoint can fulfil most needs. If you haven't got a colour printer, the colour slides, which appear on the PC screen, will be printed out in mono-chrome. PowerPoint provides the option of viewing the slides in colour and mono-chrome.

To help the new user, PowerPoint has a number of ready-made templates for your presentation material. Text and graphic material can therefore be easily aligned. There are tools within PowerPoint to enable you to use animation and video footage in a presentation. By using the **Pack and Go Wizard** you can collect all your material (pictures, images, animation files) into a stand alone format that can be stored on floppy disc for portable presentations in the field. There is also a **Meeting Minder** to allow you to make notes during the actual presentations – useful as you progress through the presentation to enhance customer understanding.

Planning with Schedule+

If you want to plan your day down to the very last minute you will find **Schedule +** very useful. It has numerous features for planning activities and scheduling events. These include:

- Calendar views (monthly, weekly and daily)
- Meeting wizard
- Contact Manager
- Daily To Do list
- Time zone display
- Autodial on your telephone
- Appointment and task lists.

If your PC is connected to a network (see Chapter 7) then it's quite possible to have your diary updated by someone else from another PC – no excuse for missing meetings, although some people would find such a feature quite intolerable. Alternatively, if you have a sound card in your PC you can use it to generate an audio announcement of imminent events in your daily schedule. And at the end of the working day you can get Schedule + to perform an automatic print out of tomorrow's diary.

Using Access

Access is Microsoft's database for Windows. Although the memory requirements are rather steep (realistic minimum of 16 Mbyte of RAM), it's a fully comprehensive package that appeals both to the novice and experienced database user. For example, there are several ready-made databases to allow the new user to gain confidence. Once confidence has been established you can evoke the **Access Wizard** that enables you to customise databases to your own needs. It does this by leading you through a set of dialogue boxes containing questions that you answer. In fact, Access provides you with all you need to generate professional looking databases.

There is also the **Table Analyser Wizard** that allows professional users to create so-called **relational databases** by collating data from several sources or tables. As with all components in the Office 97 suite, Access accommodates OLE for exchanging data with the other members of the suite.

Ask for a demonstration

You will find that other Integrated Office Suites (IOSs) offer very similar features to the above. Although no two IOSs are the same, you should have gained a reasonable impression of what an IOS has to offer and whether it is suitable for your needs. If you're looking for an IOS and you visit a local PC shop don't hesitate to ask for a demonstration of their IOSs.

WHY YOU'LL NEED OCR SOFTWARE

An application that frequently arises is to convert the words on a printed page into a document acceptable to a wordprocessor. This process can be achieved by means of **optical character recognition** (OCR) software, which will convert an image of a printed page into actual text which is then stored as a wordprocessor document. You will require a means to get the image of the printed page into your PC. The easiest way to achieve this is to use an image scanner (see Chapter 5) linked up to your PC. This is becoming a very attractive option owing to the falling prices of flat-bed scanners (less than £250).

Using OCR software

The whole process is quite straightforward. When you are ready, you invoke the OCR software and it accesses and controls the image scanner. If the page is simple text without any pictures or diagrams you simply instruct the OCR to perform the conversion. Once the page is complete the OCR will ask you for the next page. When you have finished scanning all the pages the OCR will ask for a file name and that completes the operation. If the text is laid out on the page with diagrams you can request the scanned page image to be shown on the screen. By means of the mouse you can mark off the text you want converted, thereby avoiding the diagrams. Some OCR software will even recognise text areas automatically. The whole conversion process is surprisingly quick and accurate as most OCR software has a learning algorithm to recognise characters. You will also find an option for correcting errors by means of a spell checker. You may even have recognition of the fonts on the original page. Examples of OCR software packages are **TextBridge Pro** and **Omnipage Pro**.

LOOKING AT MULTIMEDIA SOFTWARE

Chapter 3 describes the multimedia possibilities offered by the PC. However, to create a multimedia presentation or application you will require a software suite that is able to integrate text, images, sound files, video clips, animations and MIDI files. The collective term given to this is **authoring software** and there is a great deal of it on the market. Once again the old adage applies – you get what you pay for. Authoring software is not the only means of creating multimedia applications. You can access all the features of **Microsoft's Media Control Interface** (MCI – see Chapter 3) by programming with Visual BASIC or Visual C++. These are known as High Level Languages.

Choosing from a wide range

The market for multimedia products is huge and it should not come as any surprise to learn that numerous software packages are on the market for creating multimedia applications. The price range reflects the seriousness taken by the creators of multimedia authoring tools. There is a lot of software at the top end of the market (more than £1,000), and you will also find some authoring software which is a cut-down version of a larger product.

Using icons

A number of multimedia authoring tools are command line based. You have to enter written instructions as part of the programming scheme. This takes a little practice but does offer a lot of flexibility.

The alternative scheme used by many authoring tools is to use the icon drag and drop method with the mouse. An icon represents a task and copies of tasks are brought into the working area by dragging and dropping. You then link them together into a logical sequence to generate a flowchart of your requirements. The flowchart becomes in effect your program. The flowchart reflects a menu structure because the key feature is interactivity. There will be a **library** of icons to choose from; for example, icons for accessing the MCI features to play MIDI files or show video clips.

Marketing your multimedia

Your initial task will be to design your multimedia application using the icon language of the authoring software product. Once you have created a multimedia application you may have thoughts on marketing it in a CD-ROM format. Your attention should therefore be drawn to the availability of low cost CD-Rs for creating your own master CD-ROMs (see Chapter 5).

DESKTOP PUBLISHING

Over the past few years desktop publishing (DTP) has been one of the main applications of the PC. Low-cost hardware and software for generating professional looking documents have spawned a new printing sub-culture. From parish newsletters to company reports, DTP has had a beneficial effect on the creation of printed information. A PC-based DTP system requires a high performance PC, a quality DTP software package and a laser printer (see Chapter 5).

For colour DTP you will also require a quality colour printer, although relatively little printing actually requires colour. It should, however, be stressed that if you intend to perform some serious DTP work you will definitely need a laser printer to produce the final product. A laser printer will give you quality and speed of printing.

DTP features

A DTP package should offer the user a wide degree of freedom in the way text and images are laid out. In general, text and images are contained in frames which can be moved or dragged around like objects on the page. When you introduce a new frame the successive frames move along to make space for it. If, however, you have a picture, its position can be fixed while text from the frame above it will wrap around it if desired. As a user you define how many columns you require (with the appropriate spacing) and you build your page layout. You will also be able to rotate and resize each object if you desire.

Fonts

Most DTP packages come with a vast number of fonts, although you will find that most of them are quite unsuitable for anything. When you are creating a text frame you can choose the font type, size, colour and attributes (bold, italic, underline). There is, however, one important rule – do not use too many font types on a page. Four should be a maximum otherwise the page will look very messy.

Images

One important feature of a DTP package is the ease of manipulating images. As well as importing pictures (either from a file or from an image scanner – see Chapter 5) you can perform a degree of image filtering – adjusting the colours or making the pictures more clearer.

To make your documents more attractive you will also have a wealth of **clipart images** to select from. These are very useful for enhancing the visual impact of a printed page. Together with lots of headings they help to sustain the interest of the reader by breaking the text up into more manageable and digestible chunks. You will find that most commercial DTP software can import a whole variety of different image format types. There are many image formats, .TIF, .PCX, .EPS, Windows bitmap, to name just a few.

Commercial colour printing
If your work contains coloured images and you intend to produce a quality product with colour pictures, it's important that your DTP software is recognised by commercial image setters or high-end reprographics printing facilities. Colour separation is therefore essential for producing high resolution film. Before you buy ensure that this is an option.

Special effects
Every DTP package worth its salt will be able to perform special effects such as rotating text, skewing text or even generating decorative layouts like this one.

Other special effects include decorative borders, colour backgrounds and pretty patterns. You also have the opportunity to include your own drawing by using the integral DTP drawing software. However, to exploit these features to the full you need a good imagination and a lot of patience and perseverance to achieve a quality result.

Choosing commercial DTP software
There are several DTP software packages (see Appendix A) on the market and these include:

- **QuarkXPress**: commonly used by publishing houses to produce glossy magazines. It has **XPress XTensions** produced by third companies to increase its functionality.

- **PagePlus**: low cost DTP package with all the features for small scale printing applications. Has several tools for satisfying DTP needs – image editing, drawing, generating tables and producing decorative text frames. Available for Windows.

- **PageMaker**: works very well with PhotoShop which is a quality image manipulation and colour editing software package. PageMaker also deals very well with multi-chapter documents together with index and table of contents.

- **Ventura**: interfaces with CorelDraw and is ideal for applications which require the drawing of pictures (comic strips) – available for Windows.

- **FrameMaker**: well suited for books and large documents, it supports cross-referencing, indexed footnotes and automatic page numbering repagination. It also has a dictionary for spell checking.

Your choice of a DTP package will of course be dependent upon your application. If you are buying your PC primarily for DTP work then it is highly likely that you'll be looking at a software package at the higher end of the market (£600 +). Don't forget to budget for training sessions. Using a DTP package efficiently needs training and a lot of practice.

WHY YOU MAY NEED ANTI-VIRUS SOFTWARE

One of the less commendable achievements of the human imagination is the obscene invention of so-called computer viruses that can have disastrous effects upon the operation of PCs. These are the products of psychologically disturbed minds who are hell bent on causing mayhem amongst PC owners and users. A computer virus, like its biological counterpart, is a fragment of software that attaches itself to other software in the PC. It can multiply by copying itself onto other software applications in the PC. The boot sector on the hard-disc is a favourite place for viruses to reside. On a trigger event (Friday 13 is a well-known trigger event) it may destroy the data in the boot sector and consequently all the information on the hard-disc could be lost.

You will not know whether your PC has been infected by a virus until it strikes, by which time it's too late. However, help is at hand. There are a number of software applications on the market that seek out computer viruses and remove them without causing any harm to the system. Thousands of viruses have been identified and more are created every year by sick minds. Anti-virus software therefore has to be updated on a regular basis. Once it has been installed, every time the PC is powered up a check is made on all the files to see whether any virus infection has occurred.

High risk virus sources

It is relatively rare, but not unknown, for commercial software to be contaminated by a virus. If you install illicit copies of software from a floppy disc there is a greater chance of being infected. You should as a matter of course run a virus check on every floppy disc and even CD-ROM that you insert into your PC. After all, if there is a virus lurking on a floppy disc you only have yourself to blame for not taking adequate precautions.

A far more likely source of virus infection is downloading data from the Internet (see Chapter 6). There are so many sources out there and nobody knows the scale of contamination. If you are likely to use the Internet regularly to download information it would be very unwise of you not to have resident anti-virus software on your PC.

Choosing commercial anti-virus software

There are a number of software applications that are designed to seek out computer viruses and wipe them off the system. Three well-known products are **Dr Solomon's Anti-virus Toolkit**, **Norton Anti-Virus for Windows** and **McAlfee**.

CHECKLIST

- Make out a list of applications that you have lined up for your PC and try and identify what software packages you will need.

- Check with your local PC shop or stockist for the prices of the software products that you are interested in.

- Compare the prices with advertisements in PC magazines (don't forget the hidden costs of delivery and VAT).

- When you are buying a new PC and a software package make sure there's sufficient RAM in the PC to enable the software to operate properly.

CASE STUDIES

Christine has to standardise the software used by the administration in her company

Christine has been appointed as the Administration Officer of a small to medium size company which has a network of PCs. To ensure that uniformity exists between the administrative personnel she is going to install a networked version of Office 97 for which she will require a site licence. Christine will also ensure that each PC on the network has the following minimum specification:

- CPU – Pentium P166
- 1.2 Gbyte hard-disc
- 16 Mbyte of RAM
- colour monitor
- network card.

Christine has also identified a limited need for database applications. She intends to use **Microsoft's Access** and will specify that every PC that is likely to use Access will have 16 Mbyte of RAM. With a networked version of the software several users can work on the same documents at the same time. This is often necessary for large projects. Christine has also specified additional hardware:

- A laser printer (see Chapter 5) for every four users on the network.
- A network server (see Chapter 7) to hold all common data and the Office 97 software.

Martin has to give sales presentations at several venues

Martin's company has created a multimedia presentation on a CD-ROM for him to use. He has decided that what he needs is a lap-top PC which doubles up as a projector tablet for an overhead projector. Lap-top PCs normally use liquid crystal displays (LCDs).

Once mounted, the light from the overhead projector passes through the LCD of the PC and can be projected onto a large presentation screen. By connecting the personnel address (PA) system to the line-out on his PC, Martin can have a sound track with his multimedia video. Martin's PC specifications will be:

- lap-top PC with removable panel to allow mounting on an overhead projector
- integral CD-ROM drive
- integral sound card.

A PC that fulfils Martin's requirements is the **Showman** from **Xitec** (Tel: (0181) 287 4000) which make 486DX4 (100MHz) and Pentium versions.

DISCUSSION POINTS

1. Having looked at a range of software products are you able to determine what type of software is needed for your immediate needs?

2. Are you able to determine software products that you will need in the future?

3. If you intend to perform any DTP work on your PC in the future what consideration should you give to the PC's memory?

5
Adding Peripherals to your PC

In this chapter, the emphasis will be on the peripherals that can be added to the standard PC to enhance its functionality and tailor its configuration according to its intended application. This chapter will help you to decide whether each peripheral will have a role to play in your proposed application.

All peripherals come with an Owner's Manual and it's in your interest to read them. Manuals have a reputation for being badly written and difficult to understand and although they are improving this is probably still true. If you experience difficulties ring the technical support number that comes with the product. It is also worthwhile keeping a notebook of these numbers as you will probably need technical support from time to time.

LOOKING AT PRINTERS

A printer is regarded as an indispensable component for conducting any type of work. When budgeting for a new PC, serious consideration must be paid to your needs to generate printed material. There are several types of printer on the market providing a range of quality in the finished printed product. The cheapest solution is not always the best and it will be necessary for you to try and match your needs with the printer type. The following sections will help you to make a decision regarding the most appropriate type of printer for your need.

Matrix printers

The most common type of printer is the matrix printer (Figure 14), so called because the printing head consists of an array (matrix) of pins which move forward onto an inked ribbon to construct the print character. The quality of the print depends on how many pins there are in the head, 24 normally being the maximum. Although the majority of matrix printers are 80 columns (characters) for

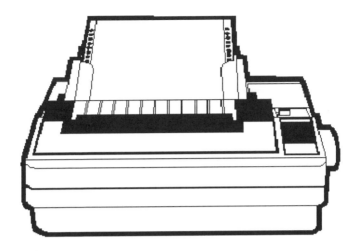

Fig. 14. Matrix printers offer low-cost solutions to many printing needs.

accommodating A4 size paper, some have a large carriage for printing 132 characters per line. Most matrix printers can accommodate perforated printer paper (using the tractor feed) – which tends to be American size – and single sheet A4.

Advantages of matrix printers
- Generally low cost and good for run of the mill printing.
- Perforated printer paper is cheap.
- Most have a number of different font features (for instance, condensed, bold, italic) which are selected either from the PC or by the front panel controls.
- Low-cost maintenance consumables – the ribbon.
- Most matrix printers are compatible with the Epson standard.

Disadvantages of matrix printers
- Printouts are tiresome to read.
- The printing rate is very slow, especially if producing non-standard characters.
- Poor at producing diagrams.
- Limited range of fonts and font sizes.
- Noisy.
- The inked ribbon needs replacing frequently.
- When printing A4 single sheets, each sheet must be fed manually.

Printing Near Letter Quality (NLQ)
One feature which is quite attractive on some matrix printers is the
option of printing to a Near Letter Quality or NLQ standard. Once
a character has been printed, a second (and sometimes third)
displaced impression is made so that the finished character does not
appear to be constructed from the dots. However, when in the NLQ
mode the print rate is greatly reduced.

Bubble jet and ink jet printers
Alternatives to the matrix printer which offer enhanced quality are
the bubble jet or ink jet printers (Figures 15 and 16) which use the
drop on demand (DOD) principle. Instead of an array of pins in the
writing head, these printers have an array (8 x 8) of nozzles. These
holes are used as jets through which ink is squirted in very small
amounts. On contact with the paper, the ink droplet blends with the
neighbouring droplets to create a continuous character and not an
impression of dots.

Fig. 15. The bubble jet printer produces very good results
but is generally quite slow.

Advantages of bubble jet and ink jet printers
- The printers are compact.
- Quiet.
- Not too expensive.
- The ink cartridges are refillable.
- The print quality is very good.

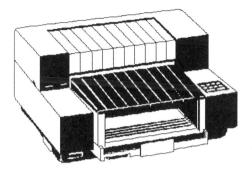

Fig. 16. The HP ink jet printer is a very popular choice
for many printing needs.

Disadvantages of bubble jet and ink jet printers
- Printing rate is slow.
- Limited number of fonts and font sizes.
- Diagram printing is only fairly good.
- Not the sort of printer to subject to a heavy printing load.

Colour printers
Over the past few years there have been several developments in
colour printing technology for small-scale PC systems. The primary
colours for colour printing are cyan, magenta, yellow and black
(CMYK). With colour printers don't expect to find the quality that
you see in glossy magazines (well, not yet). If your work requires the
production of colour prints, ask for a demonstration of each type of
printer before you decide on a particular model. There are currently
five main designs of colour printer:

- **Matrix**: this design functions in much the same way as the
  monochrome printer except there is a three or four colour ribbon
  in the colour matrix printer.

- **Liquid ink jet**: there are two types available. The first uses the
  DOD design similar to that of the monochrome ink jet or bubble
  jet printers. The second has a continuous flow where the ink is
  deflected onto the paper only if there is an electrical charge (in the
  shape of a character) on the paper, otherwise the ink passes back
  into the reservoir. There will be four reservoirs, one for each
  colour (CMYK). Quite good for 3D visualisation.

- **Thermal wax**: this design requires sheets of thermal wax, one for each colour. The paper on which the image is printed makes four passes and the printing head (an array of heated elements) presses against the wax sheet and transfers the wax onto the page. To get the best results special paper is required which matches the characteristics of the wax.

- **Dye sublimation**: not unlike the thermal wax design which uses coloured sheets. However, the impregnated dyes when subjected to the hot printing head are vaporised and then sublimate onto the printed page. This has the advantage of producing an image of continuous tone and not individual dots as with the thermal wax printers. Although the quality is reasonably good, each print tends to be quite expensive.

- **Colour laser printer**: the design is the same as the monochrome laser printer (see below) except there are four sets of mechanics – one for each colour. Although the cost per page is quite low, the price of the printer can be prohibitively high.

Colour ink jet printers

Colour printers based on the ink jet design require a special mention since their prices have dropped dramatically over the last couple of years. When selecting a colour ink jet printer make sure that it's a true CMYK – separate black cartridge from the CMY ink cartridge – otherwise you will find the print quality rather disappointing. The quality of the finished product will depend on a number of features that you should consider:

- **Paper**: for the best results you should use special paper, but this tends to be expensive. As a general rule, the better the quality of the paper the better the finished product. The printer should also be capable of handling different paper sizes and should be able to print directly onto transparencies for use with overhead projectors.

- **Printer resolution**: nothing less than 600 x 600 dots per inch (dpi). Some printers will perform up to 720 x 720 on very good quality paper – check the manufacturer's specifications.

- **Running costs**: this is a very important consideration. High quality paper is expensive and so are the ink cartridges. If you print large colour areas on your pages you will use a lot of ink – it can cost as much as £1 a page.

- Print speeds: this will depend largely on the amount of colour you have on each page. Typically do not expect more than four pages per minute (ppm). Many printers will print on average much slower than this.

Since colour ink jet printers are very attractively priced it may be advantageous to use two separate printers, a colour and a monochrome (such as a laser printer). If you choose this option you will probably need a switch adapter between your PC and the two printers unless your PC has two physical parallel printer ports. Some are automatic whereas others are manual. Examples of colour ink jet printers are the **Stylus Colour 500** from **Epson** and **Deskjet 870cxi** from **Hewlett Packard**.

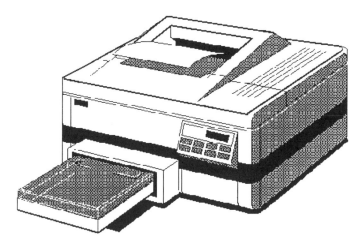

Fig. 17. Laser printers are now very affordable.

Laser printers
Over the past few years the laser printer has become an invaluable peripheral of the PC. Once it was quite rare to find a laser printer in a commercial office, but today almost every full-time secretary has her own. Once considered a luxury, laser printers are now considered as standard printing devices. The reason for this is the change in attitude by users (or buyers). The purchase of a laser printer was regarded as a substantial outlay, but once users began to

reflect on their necessity, money was forthcoming. The market duly responded by producing cheaper models. For what they are, laser printers are now very well priced and some models are available for under £400. If you are serious about your printing needs then a laser printer is a must. When drawing up your budget for a PC system you should seriously consider the inclusion of a laser printer.

Advantages of laser printers
- Very high quality printing.
- Available at modest costs (under £400).
- Excellent reproduction of diagrams and graphics.
- Can produce a large number of fonts and font sizes.
- Fast printing rate, at least six pages per minute.
- Automatic feeding of A4 size paper from paper tray.
- Has emulation features to respond as standard printers, for example HP LaserJet III or Epson FX matrix printer.
- Many have dual interfaces, serial and parallel.
- Own processing capabilities and memory. This means that the printer constructs the printed page and relieves the PC of the task.
- You can use ordinary photocopier A4 paper.

Disadvantages of laser printers
- Cost. High performance laser printers can be expensive.
- The replacement cartridge is expensive.
- Memory upgrades are expensive.
- Some models of laser printers produce ozone which can be unpleasant, although these are being phased out.
- When producing a document with a laser printer you may spend too much time on the presentation of the material at the expense of its contents!

Page descriptive language
To accommodate the vast array of fonts which are available for printing and to scale these fonts to any size or orientation, a **Page Descriptive Language** is required. The most well-known of these is **PostScript** and several laser printers host this option. Because of the high licence fee, this will add an extra few hundred £s to the cost of the printer. Some manufacturers offer the PostScript option as a cartridge module which slots into their model. However, with the clever features on the Windows **Print Manager**, it can be argued that PostScript has lost its appeal for many users and is no longer regarded as necessary.

Connecting a printer to your PC

The majority of printers will be connected to a PC via the parallel interface (previously known as the Centronics interface). When you examine the back of a PC you will see a 25-way D connector with holes (the male – Figure 18) – this is the parallel printer interface. You will need a printer cable (this can be obtained from any PC shop). The cable will have a 25-way female connector (with pins – Figure 19) on one end and a rather bulky parallel connector (with wire clips) on the other.

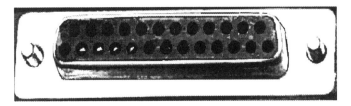

Fig. 18. The male 25-way D type connector (with holes).

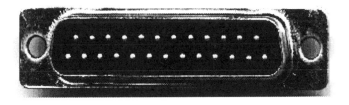

Fig. 19. The female 25-way D type connector (with pins).

Using a serial interface

On the back of the PC there will be at least two serial D connectors, a 25-pin and 9-pin females (both with pins). The 9-pin connector is usually designated COM1 whereas the 25-pin connector is designated COM2. If you wish to use the serial interface you will require a serial interface cable with the appropriate connectors (Figure 18). Some printers will have a choice of both a parallel interface and a serial interface. Ordinarily you would use the parallel interface, but if the printer is stationed several metres away from the PC you would be better off using the serial interface. If you are using the serial interface you will probably have to reset the printer to accept data along the serial link. Information on how to do this will be found in the printer's Owner's Manual.

Enhanced Parallel Port (EPP)

When specifying a new PC you should look for a parallel printer port that conforms to the American Institute of Electrical and Electronics Engineers (IEEE-1284) standard with **Enhanced Capabilities Mode** (ECM). A printer port with this specification can transfer data in excess of 1 Mega bit per second. If it supports the **Enhanced Parallel Port** (EPP) mode it will also be possible to connect it to external peripherals other than printers such as CD-ROM drives and other storage devices.

Installing a printer driver

When you buy a new PC you will have a version of Windows either on floppy discs or on a CD-ROM. Although Windows has been installed on the PC you will have to make a modification for it to recognise any new printer that you add to the system. In order for Windows to communicate with your printer you will need a **printer driver** which is a piece of software. Fortunately Windows comes with many printer drivers and it's a relatively straightforward process to install a new printer driver. Some printers come with their own driver. To install, follow the instructions in the Owner's Manual. To install the Windows driver, enter the **Settings** menu and select **Printers** and follow the instructions from there.

USING MODEM AND FAX

If your needs involve the access of data from remote sources or use of the Information Superhighway then a modem is a must (see Figure 20). It allows you to access remote services using the

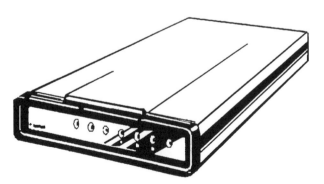

Fig. 20. An external modem. It is quite common to have modem and fax features in the same unit.

telephone line (**Public Switched Telephone Network** – PSTN). Modems come either as external units or as internal expansion cards. In general the external unit is more expensive. It is normally furnished with a lead to plug into your telephone socket and a lead that links to your PC via a serial port (usually COM2). One of the advantages of the external unit design is the set of front panel lights (LEDs) that indicate the state of the device when communication is in process. Some modems are quite sophisticated devices; not only do they provide modem and fax services but they enable simultaneous voice communication as well.

Voice modem
Some modems offer you the option of setting up a sophisticated telephone answering machine on your PC. Although a **voice modem** can act simply as an answering machine, it's possible to configure it to do far more. For example, you could be providing an information service and you may wish to leave individual messages for customers who ring you. For each customer you could allocate a unique *mail box*, containing a pre-recorded voice message. When they ring, they enter their code using the key-pad on their telephone. This enables them to access their personal mail box and receive the voice message you left for them. If you buy a voice modem you will probably get a software routine for performing this type of function. Needless to say, this facility is only available when your PC is switched on.

Understanding the specifications
Modems have a range of capabilities depending largely on cost – the more you pay the more features you get. In the world of communications there is a bewildering array of specifications and when buying a modem you will invariably encounter several of them. In the following discussion only the salient specifications of a typical modem will be covered. This should be sufficient to allow you to obtain a reasonable understanding of what's involved in modem technology. Modem transmission standards have been allocated **V numbers** from the **International Telecommunications Union – Telecommunications** (ITU-T) whose main task it is to set up standards. A quality modem is capable of operating with a number of V standards.

- **Bit rate**. Measured in bits per second (bps), this is a measure of the data transmission rate and relates to the speed at which you can receive and transmit data into and from your PC via a modem. Typical rates range from 75 bps to 56,000 bps. A good quality modem will be capable of using a number of bit rates and the choice of bit rate is dependent upon the V number used by the service you are accessing. Ideally you'll use the highest bit rate available to get the maximum rate of data transfer. It's normal for a modem to auto-detect the rate of transmission and configure itself accordingly. What normally happens when a modem commences communication is a mutual agreement on the highest acceptable bit rate. The following are the commonly used examples of the V standards often found in modems:

1. **V.32bis**, which specifies a data rate of 14,400 bps.

2. **V.34**, transmission rate of 28,800 bps and can use data compression if the system allows it.

3. **V.34bis**, transmission and receive rate of 33,300 bps, has become the standard but will be superseded by modems operating at 56,000 bps.

56,000 bps modems

High speed modems operating at 56,000 bps are becoming increasingly popular and several Internet Service Providers (ISPs) are able to transmit data at this rate. As with other modems, if the maximum data transfer rate cannot be secured it drops down to the next speed. There is, however, a problem regarding commercial 56,000 bps modems, two standards have emerged which are not always compatible:

- **X2**, this standard was set by US Robotics. Data is received and downloaded at 56,000 bps, but data in the opposite direction transmits at 33,300 bps. The X2 is ideal for Internet browsing when you want to download information from a web site. Also some modems currently operating at 33,300 bps can be upgraded to operate at 56,000 bps by loading new software into their flash memory. An example of an X2 modem is the USR Courier (Tel: 0800 225252).

- **K56 Flex**, this standard has the support of the Open 56k Forum which is an agreement between several modem manufacturers. Models which conform to the K56 Flex transmit data in both directions at 56,000 bps and it's likely that this will become the universal standard. An example of a K56 Flex modem is the Motorola 56k VoiceSURFR (Tel: (01293) 404343).

- **Data compression**. To capitalise on the full data-carrying potential of the PSTN, it is necessary to use data compression. Two standards relating to data compression are:
  1. **V.42bis**, compression of 4:1, resulting in a 9,600 baud effectively acting as a 38,400 baud.
  2. **Microcom Network Protocol** (MNP 5) which uses the Lempel-Ziv algorithm – compression of 2:1.

- **Error correction**. As data is transferred along the PSTN it frequently becomes corrupted by noise and interference in the system. One method of reducing the effect of transmission errors is to use an error correction scheme. The following types of error correction standards are often employed in modem design:
  1. V.42.
  2. MNP 2, 3 and 4.

When specifying a modem you should be able to buy one which incorporates many of the above features (and probably more) for under £200.

BABT

If you are buying a modem you should ensure that it has the BABT **Green Circle of Approval**. Do not buy or use a modem which bears the Red Triangle (non-BABT). It is illegal to use this equipment on your telephone line and you run the risk of prosecution. You also run the risk of losing your telephone connection which will invariably cause unnecessary inconvenience.

ISDN2

Using the ordinary telephone lines limits the rate of data transfer. It is in fact an analogue system and an alternative offered by the telephone companies (**BT** and **Mercury**) is the **Integrated Services Digital Network** (ISDN). The domestic or small user version is known as ISDN2 because each subscriber has two channels, each working at 64,000 bps. A user accesses it in a similar manner to that of an ordinary telephone line. Both channels are accessed simultaneously giving a data rate of 128,000 bps which can accommodate data and voice transmission. The modem standards relating to the ISDN2 requirements are known as V.110 and V.120.

One of the main advantages of ISDN2 is the possibility of implementing video conferencing (see Chapter 3) since the network has the information-carrying capacity (bandwidth) to transmit video speed data. However, it should be pointed out that the connection charges and the rental rates are quite high. The German company **Acotec** has produced an easy-to-use software interface package called **ISDN for WorkGroups** which in effect allows easy communication via BT's ISDN service between PCs which are using Windows.

Ensuring compatibility

It must be stressed that many of the services provided via the PSTN operate at bit rates of 9,600 bps or less. However, if you intend to use a modem based on the V.32bis or V.34 with software running under Windows then there may be a problem with older makes of PCs.

The data which enters the serial port of the PC must be converted to parallel data and this task is performed by a chip called **Universal Asynchronous Receiver Transmitter** or UART for short. Unfortunately the UART in older PCs only have the 8-bit 8250 or 16450 which cannot cope with the high bit rate especially when Windows is operating.

For high speed data transfer rates you will ideally need the 16-bit 16550 UART which has a 16-byte memory buffer and can accommodate interrupts from Windows. By using the msd.exe utility in Windows and clicking on the serial port option you will be able to see what UART you have in your PC. If you are buying an external modem make sure that the cable connecting the PC to the modem has all the proper connections to ensure hardware data control between PC and modem. Almost all Pentium PCs will have the 16550 UART as standard but it's worth checking just to make sure.

Buying modem software

Once your modem is in place you will require a suitable software package to communicate with your remote source. Windows has a complete utility which can function in this capacity. It operates a number of file transfer standards such as **Xmodem**, **Ymodem**, **Zmodem** and **Kermit** (after the frog), and **Bulletin Board System** (BBS) standards.

There are other software packages that perform similar functions such as **Procomm Plus for Windows** from **Datastorm**. In addition to setting up file transfer standards it also enables the modem to be configured to the user's specifications through the use of its own programming language. It will also accommodate video text graphics which are found in **PRESTEL**.

Using fax

When reviewing the many modems on the market you will probably find that many of them have fax facilities as well (a fax-modem). A fax-modem is a very inexpensive way of realising a fax facility in your PC and is strongly recommended. It can be quite invaluable as it dispenses with a lot of letter writing. Once you start using the fax card installed in your PC you will certainly notice that you buy far fewer postage stamps. A fax machine is very little more than a scanner and a modem with a hand set. The standard regarding commercial fax machines is the Group 3 (V.29) which transmits at 9,600 bps. It specifies the number of image pixel elements per scan line (pels). The Group 4 standard has a resolution which is twice that of the Group 3 but will only work with ISDN.

The majority of fax-modems will conform to what is known as the Class 3 standard and for most applications this is quite adequate. Bearing in mind that only data images are transferred with a fax facility, you may need a method to convert a page of fax text into a usable text file. This can be achieved by using **Optical Character Recognition** (OCR) software (see Chapter 4).

Buying fax software

When buying a fax-modem it is highly likely that you will have fax software bundled with the product. A well-known example of software which allows control over the fax features of a fax-modem is **WinFAX** from **Delrina**. It acts basically as a background task and makes the fax-modem appear as a printer. When working within a wordprocessor, you set up the printer as WinFAX. When the document is ready to be faxed, you click on the Print icon. A dialogue box appears and you enter the name and fax number. On clicking the Send button, the document is faxed off to its destination. WinFAX also has an optical character recognition (OCR) facility for converting received faxes into wordprocessing documents. There is also a fax utility in Windows that performs in a similar manner.

LOOKING AT PC CARDS (PCMCIA)

A range of peripheral interfaces which are growing in popularity are **PC Cards** or **Personal Computer Memory Card International Association** (PCMCIA) devices. These will be mainly of interest to users intending to buy a lap-top computer. Devices based on this standard are the same size as a credit card and a PC can be fitted with a special cradle (or socket) to accommodate the card. Its functions can be grouped as:

- **Type I**, for increasing the amount of RAM storage in a PC or just for general purpose storage such as personal records (size – 3.3 mm).

- **Type II**, for a fax/modem, mass storage, network and other peripheral devices such as a CD-ROM with SCSI (size – 5.0 mm).

In effect this means that peripheral services are interfaced to the PC through one standard interface slot. The concept of PCMCIA is particularly attractive for lap-top PCs and electronic notebooks where space is at a premium. Among the aims of the PCMCIA concept are four objectives:

- **Directly executable software**. The software in the PCMCIA card should be executable directly from the card's memory without having to load it into the PC system memory.

- **Plug and Play**. The system should be designed so that when a card is plugged in its services ought to be accessible without having to reconfigure the PC. This is a feature of Windows.

- **Host independence**. Any PC with a PCMCIA slot should be able to accommodate any other card irrespective of the manufacturer or its function.

- **Hot swapping**. You should be able to remove a card and replace it with another without having to switch off or reboot your PC.

The PCMCIA interface is certainly very attractive for users who are on the move and frequently work in remote locations. You will have to assess whether a PCMCIA interface and the services it has to offer will benefit your work.

LOADING IMAGES WITH IMAGE SCANNERS

For many applications you may want to load images into your PC. The images may be pictures or just images of pages with text on. Very often you may have a page of text which you would like loaded as a text file into your PC. One way would be to type the text in manually.

Alternatively you could use a scanner together with optical character recognition (OCR) software. This is the ideal way of transforming a page of text into a text document (see Chapter 4). One of the most effective ways of achieving this is by using an optical scanner.

Using an optical scanner

The scanner works on the principle of photographing a single thin sliver (or line) at any one time. The slivers are transferred to the PC where they are reconstituted into a file that constitutes the stored digital image of the original picture or frame. The photographic element of the scanner consists of a row or line of optical detectors. Hence when it's operating, the row of detectors effectively sweeps over the page.

Resolution

The quality of the image produced by the scanning process is dependent upon the process's resolution. This is measured in dots per inch (dpi). This is a swings and roundabout problem, for if the resolution is high, the scanning process produces a very high quality image data file but requires a lot of memory (multi-Mbyte proportions). If, on the other hand, the dpi is too low the image will be very grainy. By experimentation you will be able to determine what the optimum resolution is for your needs. Resolutions range from 75 dpi to in excess of 1,200 dpi.

Using a flatbed scanner

One design of scanner is the flatbed scanner which resembles a photocopier (see Figure 21). The page containing the image you want

Fig. 21. Flatbed image scanners are growing in popularity
due to their low cost.

to scan is placed on the scanner's glass plane and the scanner's head sweeps under the glass recording the image line by line. The data is then transferred to the PC where it is assembled into an image.

Advantages of flatbed scanners
- Because a single image can generate a very large data file, you have the option of clipping the image so that only the relevant parts of the image are scanned.
- Ideal for scanning images of A4 size or smaller.
- Scanners are available for colour or monochrome imaging.
- Adjustable resolution.

Disadvantages of flatbed scanners
- Difficult to use for pages larger than A4.
- Normally needs an SCSI (Chapter 4) interface card which is provided with the product. Some use the serial port on the PC but with this design the data transfer rate can be quite slow.

Using a handheld scanner
One alternative to the flatbed scanner is the handheld version (see Figure 22). It works on the same principle as the flatbed except the user sweeps the scanner over the image. It comes into its own when your original picture is larger than A4. The general practice is therefore to scan the original in sections and reassemble them afterwards on the PC using a suitable photo session software package.

Fig. 22. Handheld scanners are a low-cost solution for scanning images.

Advantages of handheld scanners
- Relatively low cost.
- Easy to use once you get the hang of it.
- Ideal when the original picture is small.
- Adjustable dpi setting.
- Colour or monochrome versions available.

Disadvantages of handheld scanners
- Takes an amount of practice to master the scanning technique.
- Scanning is slow, and you will need a very steady hand otherwise the image will be distorted.
- As with the flatbed scanner, an SCSI interface card is required.
- For large images you have to assemble the image sections to make a complete image – additional software required.

Using a sheet feed scanner

A design of scanner that is becoming quite popular and comes between the handheld and flatbed insofar as cost is concerned is the sheet feed scanner. It is simple to operate: the user feeds single pages into the scanner and the created image is transferred to the PC. Most of them come with an interface card that the user has to insert in the PC.

Advantages of sheet feed scanners
- Compact footprint design.
- Relatively low cost.
- Fast scanning rate – nominally 12 seconds per page.
- 300 dpi with possible interpolation to 600 dpi + .
- Convenient to use if you have a large document made from single A4 sheets that you wish to use with OCR software.

Disadvantages of sheet feed scanners
- Have to use single pages only. Not suitable for scanning magazines or books unless the pages are torn out.
- Maximum paper size A4.

Scanning magazine pictures

A word of caution: you will soon discover, when using your scanner, that you are likely to get very poor results when you scan in images from magazine pictures. You will probably find fringe patterns on the image (large blotchy tracks). These are known as **moiré fringes** and what you see is an **interference effect**. They arise because the size of the dots in magazine pictures are comparable with the resolution of your scanner. On high quality photographs the dots are much smaller than the dot size of the scanner and the moiré fringes are not visible.

Conforming to TWAIN

TWAIN is a specification which was established by a consortium of hardware and software companies for image input peripherals. TWAIN is an **application programming interface** (API) standard which is applicable to scanners, digital cameras and any other image input peripheral device. By conforming to the TWAIN standard, all these devices will require only one open industry device driver – a piece of software. Therefore, when compliant with TWAIN, a software product will be able to recognise a large number of image peripherals. When a TWAIN software product is installed on a PC, the TWAIN.DLL is loaded in the Windows directory and is used as the software interface by image generating peripherals.

Drawing pictures

There are many graphics software packages on the market and many of them are capable of performing some quite spectacular processing feats. However, if you are an artist and you want to draw pictures directly into the PC, you will need a **graphics tablet**. Although it's possible to use a mouse for drawing, the results are very crude. A graphics tablet comprises a drawing pen and tablet (a pad). The tablet is usually quite small (size of a mouse mat). As the pen is moved over the surface of the tablet a line is generated on the PC screen.

The width of the line is determined by the amount of pressure you apply with the pen – normally you can have 256 levels of pressure producing very thin to very thick lines. The tablet is linked to the PC via one of the serial ports. The colours are chosen from a colour palette conveniently placed somewhere on the screen. Examples of low-cost graphics tablets are **Acecat II** from **Capital Electronic Developments** and the **Summapad** from **Summagraphics**.

Buying an integrated peripheral system

A number of manufacturers have taken the bold step and integrated into a single unit, a printer, a fax facility and an image scanner. Instead of buying the individual units it's possible to invest in one unit that does all three functions. An example is the **Officejet** from Hewlett Packard. Although a nice idea, few will argue that it functions as well as the individual peripherals that it's meant to replace, but it is considerably cheaper and may be quite adequate for many applications.

TAKING DIGITAL PHOTOGRAPHS

It's quite possible that you may be interested in taking photographs and transferring the results to your PC. Technology has progressed to the stage where the traditional photographic film has a genuine competitor – the digital photograph. Armed with a digital camera, you can take colour images (photographs) and by interfacing the camera to your PC you can transfer the digital images directly to your hard-disc for viewing and further processing. This is particularly useful for making up photographic records – an estate agent, for example. Some digital cameras use **flash memory** which are memory integrated circuits that retain their data contents (the images) even when there is no battery power. Other digital cameras use miniature floppy discs.

Examples of digital cameras

The **QV-200** from **Casio** (Tel: (0181) 450 9131) can store 192 colour frames. The QV-200 has an integral colour liquid crystal display (LCD) screen to enable you to see not only what you are about to photograph but also the images already stored. You can even delete unwanted frames by means of its internal editor. By linking the QV-200 to a PC, via the serial interface, you can download all the images to the hard-disc as tagged image file format (TIFF) or bit mapped (BMP) files. The size of the images are 240 x 320 pixels (picture elements).

The **DC50** from **Kodak Digital Science** (Tel: (01442) 845228) can take 48 high resolution or 99 snap shot images of size 756 x 504 pixels. It has an internal memory of 4 Mbyte of RAM and uses a colour depth of 24-bits. Once the pictures have been taken they can be downloaded to a PC.

With both cameras, once stored on the hard-disc drive in the PC, the images can be manipulated with photo session software such as **CorelDraw** or **Paint Shop Pro**.

STORING DATA

If you are likely to carry valuable information on your PC then you will require a facility for backing-up your information or data. This is an absolute necessity if you have a network suite of PCs. It is common practice to copy everything on the hard-disc onto the back-up medium at the end of each working day. If something goes wrong next day you will at least have only yesterday's data to restore. There are a number of ways to achieve this. One of the commonest ways is to use a tape streamer drive back-up. This can either be an internal drive unit or an external unit. Storage capacity of QIC (quarter inch cassettes) tapes come in 420 and 850 Mbyte with a transfer rate of 9 Mbyte per minute. A low-cost external unit would connect to the parallel interface. This low-cost technology is suitable for storing modest quantities of data.

Using Digital Audio Tapes (DAT)
DAT technology is often employed in the design of back-up tape facilities and is generally more expensive than QIC tape technology. DAT drives are available as internal or external units and the storage capacity ranges from 2 Gbyte to 8 Gbyte. You will often find that DAT drives require an SCSI interface (Chapter 2) to effect fast data transfer rates.

Using a ZIP drive
A relatively new medium for storing data is the ZIP drive which is normally an external unit owing to its portable design. It uses high density magnetic discs that have a storage capacity of 100 Mbyte. In the case of the PC the ZIP drive connects via the parallel port interface.

Jaz drive
If you require high storage density an alternative technology is to use the Jaz drive which, like the Zip, has a removable disc. Available as an external or internal unit, the storage capacity of Jaz discs is 1.06 Gbyte. Jaz technology is very convenient for data storage and is likely to become the main storage medium for the music business as digital recording techniques replace traditional analogue methods. A Jaz drive will require a SCSI connection.

Storing data on erasable optical drives
Instead of using tape drives for storing data an alternative is to use an optical system or to be more precise a magneto-optic (MO) design. MO discs have read and write options and are therefore suitable for storing or archiving data that is likely to be modified in the future. Again it's available as an internal or external unit. In general the

external units can be interfaced to the PC via the parallel printer port or by using an SCSI interface card. Storage capacities range from 128 Mbyte to 1.3 Gbyte.

Using a video cassette recorder (VCR) as a backup

Probably the cheapest solution (under £40) to effect a back-up of your hard-disc is to use a **Danmere Backer** expansion card which allows your PC to be interfaced to a video recorder. The Danmere Backer card, available from **Danmere Technologies** (Tel: (01606) 44244), enables 1.5 Gbyte of data to be stored on a VHS video tape. The data transfer rate is 9 Mbyte per minute and the card is interfaced to a video recorder by two leads with RCA phono connectors.

USING A CD-RECORDER (CD-R)

A technology that is becoming very competitive is the CD-R drive (also known as the CD-recorder). With a CD-R drive you can make your own master CD-ROMs. Once you have your master CD-ROM, by using a third party duplication company, you can produce as many copies as you want. The standards laid out in the Blue Book (see Chapter 3) allow any format of information to be stored on a CD-ROM. These formats include:

- text
- images
- video (.AVI or MPEG)
- audio files
- sound files
- MIDI.

CD-Rs come in two designs, internal or external, the external option carrying a slightly higher price tag. Ideally to make a CD-ROM you should have sufficient hard-disc space available to store the **image** of the information you wish to store on the CD-ROM. The typical storage capacity of a CD-ROM is 650 Mbyte which suggests that to make the most of the CD-ROM you should have that amount of free space on your hard-disc. Although you can use multisession (copying information onto the CD-ROM in several sessions) you lose on average 16 Mbyte of CD-ROM disc space per session. Many CD-Rs write at double speed and replay at quad speed (see Chapter 3), and you can therefore use it as a CD-ROM drive. The writing time for 600 Mbyte will be just over 30 minutes (300 kbyte per second). When creating a CD-ROM the PC should be fully allocated to writing to the CD-R drive – no other tasks.

Moving a stage further from the CD-R is the CD-ReWritable or CD-RW which, as the name suggests, allows you to modify data after it has been stored on a CD-RW disc. Possessing the rewrite function CD-RW discs can be used for general data storage. An example of a CD-RW is the MP6200S from **Ricoh** (Tel: (0171) 474 1765) which also acts as a CD-R; however, to use the CD-RW facility you will require CD-erasable (CDE) discs.

Buying a commercial CD-R

An example of a low-cost CD-R is the **SureStore 4020i** from **Hewlett Packard**. It comes with an SCSI interface card and a number of software packages to help you create a multimedia CD-ROM. An alternative package, **CD Recording**, available from **CD Revolution**, comprises CD-R, SCSI interface card, **Media Styler** software and two blank CD-ROMs. However, if you are thinking about creating a professional CD-ROM you should be considering a complete multimedia authoring software package. An example is **Authorware** from **Macromedia**.

USING A UNIVERSAL SERIAL BUS (USB)

Instead of having parallel and serial ports on a PC there is a move towards using the universal serial bus (USB) which will allow users to connect up to 127 different peripherals to a PC using a single connector type. There will be no need to consider jumper settings, DMA channels, IRQ settings or I/O addresses – all this will be transparent to the user. Intel provide support for the USB standard in a number of their chipsets (see Chapter 2) and you will find that devices such as scanners, printers, modems, CD-ROMS and graphics tablets will all have a USB interface. Once a peripheral is attached to the USB it will automatically be configured as an active device.

CHECKLIST

- Judge what peripherals you require for your immediate needs. These should be included in your budget for a PC system.

- Having considered the peripherals, you will need to check that the software you intend to use is compatible with the peripherals (see Chapter 6).

CASE STUDIES

In this chapter we have outlined numerous peripherals that can be added to a PC in order to extend its functionality. We can now look at three disparate examples where the PC can be adapted to service particular requirements. These should serve to illustrate the wide-ranging diversity of the PC as a general purpose information-processing tool.

Bob wants to produce brochures for the properties on his books

Most people are familiar with the role played by an estate agent in the sale of property. When assessing the suitability of a property Bob needs to provide a brochure outlining its details for the potential buyer. A necessary part of the brochure is photographs showing various aspects of the property. This is an ideal application for a digital camera interfaced to a PC. The equipment needed by Bob will include:

- Pentium-based PC with 2.2 Gbyte hard-disc
- desk top publishing software for producing brochures (this task could be performed by a good quality wordprocessor)
- image manipulation software (for example Photoshop)
- digital camera with PC interface card
- 600 dpi laser printer for producing acceptable monochrome pictures.

Once Bob has taken the pictures, he can download them into his PC via the interface card where they can be reviewed and touched-up using the image manipulation software. The brochure can be generated using the DTP package – a standard property template would be the common method. (A **template** is a page layout that you invoke for a specific application. Wordprocessors come with several templates such as diary layout for the day.)

The pictures can be imported into the brochure at any stage and manipulated to fit the template. Once complete, the 600 dpi laser printer will produce the finished product. Although it would be preferable to have colour pictures in which case Bob could consider an ink jet colour printer.

Glenys wants her PC to perform fax operations

Glenys is responsible for ordering in her company. She will soon learn that one of the most useful peripherals to have with her PC is a fax card. As mentioned above, it is commonplace to have a fax and modem in the same unit. These can either be external or internal expansion cards. Glenys's requirements will include:

- Pentium based PC with 2.2 Gbyte hard-disc and 16 Mbyte of RAM.
- Wordprocessor running under Windows.
- Modem/fax external unit or internal expansion card. The external unit will require a power supply and a lead to connect it to a free COMM port on the PC.
- Fax software – supplied as standard with Windows. This is configured as a printer. Select Printer from the printer set-up and when you want to fax the document click on the printer icon in the wordprocessor. It will then ask for a fax number and away you go.

A record of all Glenys's faxes will automatically be kept on her hard-disc. She can also configure the fax software to answer on a specified number of rings. It will then indicate that a fax has been received.

Roger needs his lap-top to communicate remotely with his office PC network

Roger meets many customers during his working day as a salesman and he needs fast quotes for items from his company's product range. As stated above, many lap-top PCs come equipped with a PC card interface and there are many peripherals which incorporate this design. To realise a remote link to a main PC network facility, Roger will need to specify:

- Pentium lap-top PC with PCMCIA interface
- portable modem also with PCMCIA interface card
- mobile telephone – preferably on a digital network because it has lower noise compared with analogue networks
- network software installed on the lap-top PC (Windows).

In effect, when the remote link is made with the office PC, Roger will be treated as a normal PC user on the network.

Brian wants to produce comic strips for a magazine

Using a PC to draw pictures has never been easier or cheaper. There are lots of low-cost peripherals on the market that Brian can use to achieve his aim. Typically he will need:

- Pentium P133 PC, 32 Mbyte RAM and 3.2 Gbyte hard-disc (pictures usually require a lot of hard-disc space).
- Graphics Tablet with touch sensitive pen to produce varying thickness lines.
- Suitable drawing software such as Corel Draw which is one of the most comprehensive drawing packages on the market.
- Colour bubble jet printer to produce draft outputs. Normally publishers accept disc files with the images on as the print quality of magazines is much better than that produced by low cost printers.

Brian will find that the Graphics Tablet will require a certain amount of practice and also getting used to the features on the drawing software will take time.

DISCUSSION POINTS

1. Having considered the range of printer technologies available, investigate which type of printer will be the most appropriate for your immediate needs.

2. Try and make a realistic assessment of your future needs for data back-up. Remember, if you are likely to accumulate a lot of material on the PC's hard-disc you will need an external storage facility.

3. Make an assessment of the potential uses if a fax facility is added to your PC.

6
Accessing the Internet

One aspect of PC technology that has grown in significance over the past few years has been the Internet (or the Information Superhighway as it is sometimes known). The Internet is a vast network of computers scattered throughout the world that, given the right facilities, you can access via your telephone line for a premium cost. It is instructive to think of the Internet as a very large information source and also a medium to allow you to communicate with like-minded people throughout the continents. The Internet is not the only source of information; there are a number of companies that have specialised databases that you have to pay for if you require access. There are also **Bulletin Board Services** (BBS) that are normally free (see below), although the amount of information available is very much subject dependent. When you are accessing any service via your telephone line don't forget that you have to budget for increased telephone bills.

The information in this chapter should act as a guide to help you buy the appropriate services to enable you to access the Internet. For greater detail see *Using the Internet*, by Graham Jones in this series.

USING A MODEM

In order to maximise the full potential of the Internet your PC system should have the following features:

- Pentium PC (see Chapter 2).
- High quality PC graphics to view Internet image information (see Chapter 3).
- Modem, either V.32bis or better still V.34. An external modem is easier to set up than an internal modem expansion card, although with Windows PnP (see Chapter 4) this should not be a problem.
- 16,550 UART on comms serial port connected to the modem (see Chapter 5).

- Suitable Internet software (see below).
- Contract with commercial Internet Service Provider (ISP).

An important medium through which information for research can be accessed is the Public Switch Network (the telephone link). This is achieved by installing a modem in your PC. Modems and their technology have been covered in detail in Chapter 5. Once a modem is in place in your PC you will be able to access a variety of information sources through your telephone line. There are a number of software packages that make the access of remote information sources easier, and these will be discussed in this chapter. Information sources can be divided into three categories:

- commercial online services
- Bulletin Board Services
- the Internet.

We shall only deal very briefly with the first two in this list.

Using commercial online services
There are several commercial sources which provide data for a large variety of fields. Much of these data are of a specialist nature; for example, the current state of shares on the **London Stock Exchange**. In general, most of these companies permit its subscribers to access a range of databases. There are many tens of databases and you will find that several companies access the same ones. As a subscriber you pay an annual charge and an hourly rate as you use their services.

Accessing via a gateway
In general, it is possible to access the databases of one company by means of a **gateway** from another, a service that many online retailers offer. However, many of these services are expensive, and you should only use them if you have a well-defined need for them. Many of these information retail companies also offer training sessions on their systems which ensure that the customers make efficient use of their services.

Using Bulletin Board Services
The easiest facilities to access with your modem are the Bulletin Board Services (BBS) and these are usually free. In general, most BBSs provide specialised information. Many companies operate a

BBS in support of their market line of products; for example, the American chip manufacturer Motorola publishes application notes on its range of microprocessors. Many of the application notes have software listing. Instead of copying out the software, Motorola has made available a BBS which enables users to transfer (download) the software directly to their own PC.

The BBS has also become a valuable tool for manufacturers to provide customer support. With the increasing degree of complexity in high-tech products, many companies are using BBSs to make available information to help resolve customers' technical queries. Once you start roaming among professional BBSs you will become aware that much of the information on them comprises advertisements to indicate **what's on offer**. You may even be expected to pay a fee when requesting more information at a future date. For example, **Sound Blaster** (the makers of sound cards) have a BBS and the number is (01734) 344080. In general, though, most companies, and some individuals, have their own web sites instead (see below).

UNDERSTANDING THE INTERNET

The Internet is regarded as an international array of computer nodes which are connected by means of superhighways for digital information transfer. Irrespective of the source or destination computer platform designs, which may be totally incompatible (mainframes or mini computers or whatever), Internet is a means to effect data exchange across the continents. The Internet therefore consists of a network of computers, some of which are responsible for routing packets of data across an international network of computers. The information on the Internet covers almost everything, academic, entertainment, personal exchange and commercial. Of a more controversial nature, the Internet has become a source of pornographic material.

Becoming a subscriber

You gain access to the Internet by subscribing to one of the many commercial Internet Service Providers (ISPs). The well-known ones are CompuServe, CIX and Pipix. The service company will probably provide you with the necessary Windows software packages to enable you to **surf the Internet**. For example, CompuServe will provide a browser software package called **WinCIM**. To make life that little more interesting you can add **Voice E-Mail** to it to enable sound files (.WAV) to be transmitted.

Before we get onto the actual ISPs let's consider what the Internet has to offer.

Using Internet services

The Internet has several services which allow you to access its resources and make efficient use of the information available. It is likely that you'll want to read information sent to your PC and also to store it using a download facility. Whatever communication software you use when accessing the Internet you will be able to download any type of data, whether it's images, sound files, video or whatever. If you are likely to download a lot of information you should be using a V.34 modem or at least a V.32bis modem (see Chapter 5) with your PC to enable maximum data transfer – you will be charged by the hour and time is money. Here are some of the facilities that an Internet service provider will make available.

Telnet

Allows a user to access remote computers and use them interactively. The range of services that you will be able to access will depend upon the level of your entry and your associated access rights. File retrieval can be accomplished by using the **File Transfer Protocol** (see below).

Usenet

This is basically a system of discussion groups which use the Internet to disseminate information and news. The news groups are partitioned into a hierarchy of sub-groups depending on the subject matter. Usenet is now a recognised means for commercial organisations to make known information regarding their performance. It's also used as a channel for issuing press releases internationally, especially in the USA. If you are likely to access Usenet you may come across the **Network News Transfer Protocol** or NNTP.

Gopher

This is a facility to help the user navigate through the Internet's resources. By means of a menu the user defines the subject area of interest and Gopher performs a low-level search for information on the subject. The information can be read, downloaded to the user's PC or sent to the user's email address.

Archie
This is a facility for finding the location of a named data file or database. It can even be used for finding a number of files with common names. Once a search has commenced you no longer have to remain **online** (connected) with Internet. By using email (see below), once the search has been completed a message will be left for you with the information you require.

FTP
This stands for **File Transfer Protocol** and relates to the method used to transfer and retrieve files from remote computers on the Internet. With an FTP Server (a software utility) you can set up your own site on the Internet as a source of information.

World Wide Web
Also known as **WWW** or **W3**, giving a graphical view of the Internet, it is an Electronic Book, a hypertext-based facility for exploring stored information. When a PC is equipped with suitable **browser** software, such as **Explorer** (from Microsoft) or **Netscape**, it is possible to operate hypertext access. For example, you may be reading about population growth in Bangladesh and the highlighted word climate appears in the text. By clicking on the word 'climate', you may enter another database which contains information on Bangladesh's weather systems. By this means it is possible to explore a whole web of information regarding a particular research interest. Another attractive feature of W3 is the provision for accessing image and sound files. When you become familiar with the W3 format you frequently come across addresses of the sort:

> http://WWW.___.___.___.

You have what is known as web sites which are specialist sites that you can visit to obtain information that is likely to be of interest to you. There are thousands of web sites on the Internet. During your visit you can download information to your PC's hard-disc, text files or images.

Off Line Readers (OLRs)
OLRs are a means to reduce your costs by allowing you to download information and read it at a later time when you are not actually connected to the ISP. It is particularly useful for dealing with

information from the news service Usenet. CIX provide an OLR called Amerol.

Search Engines

Once you are on the Internet a very convenient method for searching the myriad of WEB sites is to use a **search engine** (a software facility). You enter the key words of your search and the search engine will find *all* the WEB sites where the word combination is found. Search engines also have facilities for fine tuning your search. Examples of a search engine are AltaVista and Yahoo. These should be available from your ISP.

Using email

One of the principal services of Internet is electronic mail or email. It is now a well-established method of communication between peers and groups of peers. It is a convenient medium for transferring messages, text, images and software (binary files). The advent of email allows international discussion groups to be set up and operate albeit in a rather slow fashion. The majority of users of the Internet are connected via a commercial organisation providing online services. They charge a monthly rate and premium for accessing Internet. They also provide storage facilities (pigeon holes) for their customers' email. When an email message is sent to you it is logged in the file servers of your access company until you are ready to read it.

Understanding email addresses

Email addresses which are attached to all data for transmission have a name followed by a domain, separated by the @ symbol. The domain address may have an abbreviated name of the Online service company, the nature of the institution (**gov** for government, **edu** for education, **mil** for military, **org** for other organisation or **net** for network resources) and the code for the country (**uk** for example). Instead of using real-time information retrieval, which can be expensive, it may be more appropriate to use the email facility. Once the information is available, a message is left for you in your email directory and you can transfer the information (download) whenever you want.

Using Internet software suites

At one time most of the functions mentioned above could only be realised by using several software utilities. However, today there are several integrated network software suites containing utilities that perform all of the above tasks and much more. A number, available in the UK, are listed below. As an example we can take a closer look at the features in a typical package – **Pipex Dial**. Like the others it runs under Windows and it's available on CD-ROM.

- **WWW Browser**: uses Netscape which can be configured to your own needs, although the default settings are quite acceptable.

- **Email**: comprises the Mail-It utility that conforms to the MIME and MIMI standards and uses the Post Office Protocol (POP) mailbox for receiving and sending mail. It also has an address book and a folder for storing email.

- **FTP**: controlled by a directory utility which employs mouse drag and drop for the transfer of files.

- **Usenet News**: news groups are read with the aid of the Netscape browser which functions as an online (while you are connected) feature, although Usenet information can be saved on disc.

- **Telnet**: enables you to log into remote computers; multiple Telnet sessions can be accommodated.

- **Ping**: a diagnostic utility to help identify faults if they occur in your Internet voyage.

This should serve as an example of what to expect when you start using Internet software.

Browsers

With the growth of web sites on the Internet a user will require a browser facility to make effective access of everything on offer. There are numerous browsers available including **Explorer** from Microsoft and **Navigator** from Netscape. To give an indication of what to expect from a browser we shall take a closer look at Netscape Navigator.

Netscape Navigator

This product has numerous facilities including the following features:

- LiveAudio: allows you to play embedded audio files from web pages.

- LiveVideo: allows you to play .AVI video footage that is embedded in web pages.
- Live3D: allows you to enter virtual reality 3D animations created by so called Mark-up languages.
- CoolTalk: a conferencing facility with three features, an Internet telephone, a Chat line (using the keyboard) and a White-board. The Chat line splits the PC screen into two sections, the upper section for the online dialogue (what your respondent sends) and the lower section with your note pad (what you send). The White-board allows you and your respondent to draw figures, using the mouse, on each other's screen.
- LiveConnect: allows so called **plug-ins**, which are add-on software features developed by Netscape and third party companies, to be integrated smoothly into Netscape Navigator. Plug-ins have the effect of enhancing the functionality of the product.

INTERNET SERVICE PROVIDERS (ISPs)

There are numerous companies that act as ISPs and the range of services they offer tend to vary from company to company. There are two broad services they offer and it's important to distinguish between them.

- **Direct access to the Internet**. The ISP will provide you with Internet protocol (IP) which allows you direct access to all the features on the Internet without restriction. This option offers the greatest flexibility.
- **Gateway access**. The ISP provides a gateway through which all your information transfer has to flow. This gives a simple front end and is easy to work with. This used to be the traditional method of reaching online services. Gateway access can be slower than IP since information is first transferred to the gateway and then to its destination.

Some ISPs can offer both, but if you are likely to become an extensive user of the Internet the gateway option is probably not for you. Either way the ISP will charge you a signing up fee, a monthly fee and additional costs depending on the extent to which you use the service. This information should be clear in their sales brochure.

Accessing ISPs

To gain access to an ISP, you can request details via fax or by telephone. The information pack will provide all the necessary details and may contain some software to get you started. Alternatively you can invoke the terminal program in Windows and dial the appropriate number. When the ISP comes on line the screen will fill up with text asking who you are. If you are going to subscribe to their services they will probably ask you for a credit card number on which they will charge their services. It is somewhat disconcerting to be asked for a credit card number so soon after logging on.

Below is a list of some ISPs in the UK – inclusion in the list is not meant to imply recommendation, merely to provide initial information for the reader. Selecting an ISP will depend on the range of services each offers. Their costs and what they have to offer will be found in their sales brochure. You will find a variation in monthly costs as well as rental expenses. Make sure you read the fine print carefully and try to select an ISP that provides the service closest to your current needs. Having to pay for lots of features that you are not likely to use is money wasted – your IP will cost enough anyway.

Internet Service Provider	Telephone No.
IBM Global Network	0990 466 466
CompuServe	0990 000 020
Which Online	0645 830 256
Pipex Dial	0500 474739
Virgin Net	0500 55 88 00
Global Net	0181 957 1026
Microsoft Network	0345 002000
Konect	0171 345 7777
LineOne	0800 111 210

WHAT'S ON THE INTERNET?

The Internet offers a variety of services that can be broadly grouped as:

- exchanging information with other like-minded people
- retrieving information from a database
- accessing interactive services such as shopping and banking.

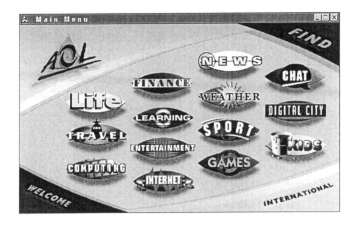

Fig. 23. The AOL Main Menu: by mouse clicking on any of the
icons you access their services directly.

On the Internet there are thousands of different discussion groups,
all having a bewildering range of interests. Whatever your interest
you will be able to find an interest group with which you have
something in common. Many of the discussion groups are of an
academic nature and you will find many knowledgeable people
contributing to them.

Using WWW you can visit web sites whenever you like and you
will find that the information on offer relates to specific interest
groups. When you subscribe to an ISP you will be provided with the
software needed to access the services they have on offer. For
example the AOL software (shown in Figure 23) allows you to
explore the various services they have. You can therefore interrogate
their information sites with relative ease. However, one of the most
frustrating things that you will find is the amount of time you spend
waiting for pages to be downloaded to your PC. Some newspapers
and magazines in the UK and America have web sites, for example:

The Times: http://www.the-times.co.uk
The Sunday Times: http://www.sunday-times.co.uk
The Electronics Telegraph: http://www.telegraph.co.uk
The Guardian: http://go.guardian.co.uk
The Financial Times: http://www.usa.ft.com/
ABC: http://www.realaudio.com/contentp/abc.html

CNN Interactive: http://www.cnn.com/
The Virtual Times: http://www.virtualtimes.com
The Economist: http://www.economist.co.uk
Time Out: http://www.timeout.co.uk

How to avoid waiting

Although the phrase **surfing the net** is often used, it's very far from the everyday understanding of fast. To maximise the transfer of data you should acquire a modem operating at 56,000 bps or at least 36,000 bps. However, the response of any web site will depend on how heavy the traffic is – the number of other users on the same route. Most activity on the Internet takes place in the USA and you will find that access to the Internet is much faster when the USA is sleeping– they are between six and eight hours behind UK time.

Sources of information on the Internet

This chapter contains only a fragment of information relating to the Internet or Information Superhighway. It has become a subject of considerable interest and in your local bookshop, if it has a computer book section, you will find many books on Internet related matters. Most of them are of American origin and are generally quite expensive, so you are advised to choose carefully before buying.

CHECKLIST

- Make sure that the ISP you sign up with is able to offer all the services that you need.

- Check the prices for each of the ISP companies that you are considering. There is quite a variation in price.

- Look out for hidden prices as some of the facilities on offer cost extra. Make sure you are aware of these before you sign up.

CASE STUDY

Peter requires a PC to perform searches of web sites

Using a PC to access the Internet to visit web sites is a relatively straightforward task to perform. Peter's minimum requirements will be:

- Pentium P166 PC with SVGA graphics and mouse.
- 2.2 Gbyte hard-disc, probably needed to download images which are memory intensive.
- Fast serial port with a 16,550 UART (see Chapter 5).
- V.34bis or V.34 modem (external or internal) with a suitable software driver (see Chapter 5).
- Windows, which will probably have a software driver for the modem which is selected when the modem is installed.
- Contract with an Internet Service Provider (ISP) usually made with a credit card.

In fact, any modern PC that has a 16,550 UART serial port will suffice for this task. Peter will have to make sure that he dials into a service that recognises the V.34 (28,800 bps) or better still V.34 bis (36,000 bps – see Chapter 5) otherwise he will spend a lot of time waiting for the transfer of information. This set of requirements is valid for anyone who wishes to perform Internet searching or surfing.

DISCUSSION POINTS

1. Before you make a contract with an ISP make a list of the services that you want from them, then consider whether you think it is cost effective to take out a subscription with them.

2. Think of the various ways that you may use the information that you are likely to obtain from the sites that you visit.

3. Do you think that the company you work for would benefit from having its own web site?

7
Defining a Small PC Network

If you have a facility where there is more than one PC in use, whether it's in a school, an office or even in the home, then there are several advantages in connecting the PCs together to form a network. At one time a Local Area Network (LAN) was a complicated affair, but fortunately those days are well past and today it's relatively easy to network two or more PCs together.

WHY HAVE A NETWORK?

When PCs are networked they effectively become a single system with several parts. Whatever is available on one should also be available on the others. For example, if you have three PCs and you want a fax facility, only one PC need have a fax unit (or fax expansion card) since all the other PCs can access it directly. This concept is referred to as **shared resources**. You can thus have several PCs and only one set of peripherals. All the peripherals will appear as if they are connected to each PC. This principle applies not only to peripherals but also to software. If there are several users of a wordprocessor package only one copy of the software is needed, as each PC can call it up as required. However, if this is the case a multi-user **site licence** for the software will be required.

Sharing with ease
It's not only the hardware features that are shared but also the data. For example, there could be two or three people using and entering data into a database. The database can be accessed and updated by all who are currently using it. Only one PC will have the actual database but all the users will have access to use it as required.

Let's look at the advantages and disadvantage of networking PCs together.

Advantages

- Any PC can access the peripherals in the system, only one printer will be needed.

- Only one copy of a software package needs to be purchased.

- It is easy to keep track of the current software on the PC.

- It is easy to access common data files – wordprocessor, spreadsheet and database files.

- When upgrading software, you only need change it on one PC.

- Several people can be working on the same project and can have equal access to the project material.

- Levels of security can be introduced to limit access to specific users.

- Today's network software is very well behaved and requires relatively little maintenance.

- Adding new features to a network can be accomplished with ease.

- Performing a back-up of all the system data will ensure that the system can be recovered if information is accidentally erased or lost through hardware failure.

Disadvantages

- Each PC must have its own network expansion card which will incur additional cost.

- Managing a network is a little more difficult than managing single PCs.

- If something goes wrong with the network all the PCs go out of action.

- Someone will have to act as the network manager to solve problems when they arise.

- He/she will also have to perform a system back-up at the end of each day.

- As more machines and facilities are added to the system the level of sophistication will increase accordingly.

- On some software packages, site licences can be expensive.

Having considered the advantages and disadvantages of networking, at the end of the day even if there are only two PCs it's actually worth networking them.

CONSTRUCTING A PC NETWORK

The configuration of a network will depend on what you want from it and the amount you are willing to spend on it. A simple configuration will comprise a few PCs in a workgroup and that's it. A more complex network, which is more expensive, will require a number of PCs and a **file server**.

Workgroup network (peer to peer)

This is the simplest configuration to construct and also by far the cheapest. If you have a number of PCs in an office or workplace they can be networked to form a workgroup. The concept of a workgroup was advanced by Microsoft's Windows. To set up a workgroup you will require:

- a network expansion card in each PC
- a coaxial network cable to connect each PC
- a BNC T-piece connector on each network card (see Figure 26)
- a coaxial 50 ohm terminator attached to the BNC T-pieces on the first and last PC in the chain.

Fig. 24. A workgroup network of PCs.

Details of the hardware features are given later on in this chapter. A typical workgroup is shown in Figure 24 and this set-up is ideal for file and program sharing. Even if you want to upgrade software it can be performed on one PC and passed onto the others in the workgroup. It should be stressed that if you only have a single user licence for a software product only one PC at a time should be using it. In principle each peripheral on any one PC can be accessed by all the others. This means that only one printer will be needed and possibly only one fax card – queues are easily set for these type of peripherals. However, there may be some limitations if several users attempt to work on the same data file at the same time. For example, common databases are often updated by several users. There will be problems when trying to do this on a workgroup network. An alternative configuration employs an **Ethernet hub** which is discussed later on in this chapter.

Relying on expertise
When trying to network two or three PCs together using Windows it is highly likely that you will encounter a few problems. You are strongly recommended to buy the PCs from a reputable dealer who specialises in and is fully conversant with networking small systems. Alternatively get to know someone who has experience of networking. Do not be surprised if it takes a lot of time and effort to get the network set up properly according to your requirements.

File server network (client/server)
A network of PCs may comprise a server and a number of PCs linked to a file server PC. The server will contain the network software and the software that each user on the network will need to access. The important point to remember is that there is no fixed design in the configuration of a small network. Most configurations can be accommodated. For example, Figure 25 shows a typical set-up with one PC acting as a server and the remaining three as nodes. This design can support four users at any one time. The only difference between the server PC and the other PCs in the network is the amount of memory in the server. Normally the server PC will have at least 64 Mbyte of RAM and a 6 Gbyte Mode 4 hard-disc

Fig. 25. A network of three PCs (nodes) and a file server.

(see Chapter 2). The server PC will also have a back-up facility such as a tape drive or a DAT (see Chapter 5). The server and the PCs are linked together by means of a coaxial cable which will be attached to a network card.

Owing to the power of modern PCs and their large hard-disc storage capacity there has been a general move away from the use of file servers for small networks.

SELECTING NETWORK HARDWARE

The only additional peripheral you have to add to your PCs to enable a network to be realised is a network card which is inserted into one of the expansion slots in the PC.

The network card

There are many different makes of network cards on the market and prices range from £20 upwards. Many cards are of the ISA design (see Chapter 2) and in most cases are quite adequate if the traffic between PCs is not likely to be very great. The cost will reflect the data transfer rate and the level of sophistication of the system. When specifying a network card for a PC running Windows you should ensure that it's **Plug and Play** (PnP – see Chapter 4) compatible. When Windows sees one of these cards the PC will automatically reconfigure itself to accept the new card. A PnP compatible card will reduce the possibility of conflict problems occurring.

PCI network card

If you are buying PCs furnished with the PCI expansion bus (see

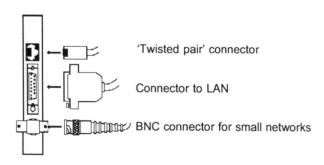

Fig. 26. Connections on a typical network PC expansion card. In a small network the BNC cable would be used to link each PC in a chain.

Chapter 2) try to ensure that the network cards are also PCI. The rear of a typical network card could have up to three connectors (as seen in Figure 26). The first is a twisted pair connector (known as an RJ-45), the same as that found on a telephone (not to be connected to the telephone though). There are two varieties: the **Unshielded Twisted Pair** (USP – also known as 10Base-T) and the Shielded Twisted Pair (STP) – the latter is less likely to be susceptible to electrical interference. The second connector (the 15-way D-connector) is used if the PC is to be linked to **Ethernet Local Area Network** (LAN – TBase-5). The third is used for a small network of PCs cascaded in a chain. It is known as the Ethernet TBase-2. It is important, but not essential that the network cards should all be the same as this minimises problems of incompatibility.

Coaxial cables
Coaxial cables are used to link the PCs in the chain and each PC will need a BNC T-piece (see Figure 26) attached to the BNC connector to enable the linking. The server (on one end of the chain) and the last PC in the chain will require a 50 ohm terminator. When searching for the hardware for a small network you may find several expansion cards in a single package. Typical suppliers, not only of network cards but also of cabling, T-pieces and terminators, are large office equipment retailers. Computer consumable suppliers have also moved into the supply market for network equipment – **LAN Warehouse** for example (Tel: 0800 248000).

Using an Ethernet hub
Using a coaxial cable to link the PCs together is an attractive means of realising a network. There is, however, one disadvantage: if the link is broken the network ceases to function. An alternative low-cost solution is to use a **hub**. This is essentially a box somewhat smaller than an A4 page that contains several bridging circuits to allow the PCs to network. Normally it will have a minimum of eight UTP or STP RJ-45 sockets. Twisted pair cable connections are therefore made between the PC's network cards and the Ethernet hub. Once the PCs are connected to the hub networking can begin after they have been successfully configured. An example of a commercial hub is the **Ethernet 10Base-T Kit** from **Addtron Technology Span Ltd** (Tel: (01494) 440500).

Uninterruptable power supplies
One problem when working with PCs is the effect of the mains

power suddenly switching off – power failure. The result is normally a complete loss of current data. For example, if you are working on a wordprocessor and have written 2,000 words, if you haven't saved your text and the power goes off you lose it all. Even if you do update (save) regularly you will still lose data if the power goes off. This can be a severe problem if there are several people working a network. The loss of one person's data is bad enough but the loss of several persons' is expensive. To avoid this problem it is common-place to use an **uninterruptable power supply** (UPS).

A UPS has a set of internal batteries and is positioned between the mains supply and your PC(s). If the mains suddenly switches off, the circuitry in the UPS senses the power loss and instantly switches over to the batteries so that the power to the PC is maintained. This will give you enough time (several minutes at least) to perform the appropriate back-up and an orderly power down of the PCs without any loss of data.

LOOKING AT NETWORK SOFTWARE

If you are intending to have more than two PCs in your network you will require network software to ensure that all the software and hardware resources are shared appropriately. At one time the installation and use of network software resembled a mini nightmare. However, today things are much improved and there are a number of software packages on the market that will render the whole process of installing a network quite painless.

Microsoft Windows and Workgroups

If you are using Windows you will be pleased to know that all the software you need to establish a workgroup network comes with Windows. With Windows you will find it a straightforward task to set up the workgroup. After the network card has been installed in your PC, on power-up Windows will perform an automatic search for the new card and will reconfigure itself accordingly after the card has been recognised. By having a PnP card this task is much easier and Windows should be able to identify the make and model of the card as well. To help you with the set-up, Windows has a Network Wizard (see Chapter 4 for Wizards). This will run you through a number of options to identify the network card (if necessary) you've installed and how you want the PC to be accessed on the network.

Novell NetWare

If you are intending to use a file server on your network with several PC nodes it may well be worth considering a comprehensive network software package such as **Novell NetWare** (Tel: (01344) 724000). Starting at around £1,000 Novell NetWare has all the management services for multiple user network communication. These include: filing, printing, common directories, security and information routing. To gain practice with the Novell NetWare a free version is available on CD-ROM which limits the number of PCs to two. It does, however, give a feel for what Novell networking is all about.

Getting expert advice

A discussion of large network systems is beyond the scope of this book but it must be stressed that if you are intending to go along this route you will require careful and considered advice. Setting up and specifying a multi-node network for numerous data-processing tasks is not easy. Be careful in your choice of suppliers: make sure that they are able to offer expert knowledge when things begin to go wrong and maintenance as and when it's needed. Sadly there are many cowboys out there who are only too willing to sell you the network system, take your money and then abandon you once the problems start.

CHECKLIST

- Check on the cost of site licences for the software you intend to use on the network. Is it cheaper to buy several copies of the software or a single site licence?

- Confirm with the company from which you are buying the network expansion cards that they are compatible with the version of Windows you intend to use. If you are going to use Windows you will find a list of recognised network cards by accessing the Network Wizard. If you intend to add a peripheral to the network, ensure that the software that comes with it enables the peripheral to be accessed by the other PCs on the network.

CASE STUDIES

You have to be careful when selecting hardware and software for networking PCs. These case studies highlight some of the problems that you will need to consider. It should be emphasised again that it's highly likely that difficulties will arise even for a small workgroup.

Fred wants to update and network the five PCs in his office

The current PCs in the office are old 386 models and Fred has been allocated a budget to buy five new PCs to form a workgroup network. He will therefore require:

• Pentium P166 with Plug and Play (PnP) based PCs, 850 Mbyte hard-disc drives and SVGA colour monitors.
• PnP network expansion cards with BNC connectors.
• Four coaxial cables, five T-pieces and two BNC 50 ohm terminators.
• Windows which has the software utilities to support workgroup networking.

Once the PnP network cards have been inserted into the PC, Windows will recognise them and reconfigure itself. Every time the PCs are powered up they should automatically search for other PCs in the group. Fred will probably have to do some tweaking using the Network Wizard in Windows to ensure that resource sharing is enabled. All this information can be found in the Network Wizard Help.

John is going to network 20 PCs and install a file server

John's task of networking a large number of PCs with a file server into a Local Area Network (LAN) is really a task for a network manager and requires a certain specialist knowledge. Typically John should be looking at:

• Identical Ethernet expansion cards for all the PCs.
• File server specifications: Pentium PRO 266 with PnP, 54 Mbyte of EDO-RAM, 6 Gbyte hard-disc with SCSI-2 interface, Ethernet network card with PCI bus and back-up tape streamer (DAT – see Chapter 5). Network software such as Novell NetWare.
• Network hardware to implement Ethernet LAN.
• Uninterruptible power supply for all PCs, especially the file server.
• Hub.

This case study serves to illustrate that setting up a LAN is not an easy task and should not be considered lightly. As stated above John would be wise to solicit the services of a network expert.

DISCUSSION POINTS

1. What are the benefits that your company would gain by networking its computers together?

2. If your PC was networked with others in the office, how do you think it would affect your working practice?

3. If your PC is part of a workgroup, will you feel comfortable when other people access your data files without you having knowledge of it?

Appendix A
Commercial PC Software

The range of commercial software for the PC is quite enormous and is expanding every day. This Appexdix will only cover a relatively small fraction of what software is available. This list is by no means a recommendation, but more of an indication of what's available in a selected range of applications. For a near complete listing of available software refer to: The Chest Software Directory, University of Bath. Tel: (01225) 826658.

The information given below is as accurate as is possible at the time of writing. Products, companies (or distributors) and telephone numbers will change over time.

Accountancy, business and tax

Pegasus Capital	Pegasus Software	(01536) 495195
WinForecast Professional	PASE	(01890) 771244
QuickBooks	Intuit	(0181) 990 5500
TAS Books	Megateck Software	(0181) 874 6511
PAGEultra	Atlantic Coast PLC	(01297) 552222
Navision Financials	Navision UK	(0181) 446 1458
Business Plan	PlanIT	(01675) 466467
Agresso	Ampersand	(01275) 374477
Dream	Squaresum	(01937) 580550
Access Accounts	Access Acounting	(01206) 322575
Smartstream Financials	Dun & Bradshaw	(01494) 424447
Dynamics C/S	Kewill Systems	(01932) 248328
Peoplesoft Financials	Peoplesoft	(01734) 522000
Renaissance CS	Ross Systems	(01734) 758181
Finance/Progress	Exact Software	(0181) 572 7718
Taxability Pro	Digital Open Systems	(01395) 270273
QuickTax	Intuit	(0181) 990 5500
TaxCalc	Which? Software	0800 252100
Paye Master	Freeway Software	(01257) 472006

Antivirus

Norton AntiVirus	Symantic Ltd	(01628) 59222
Dr Solomon's	S&S International	(01296) 318700
VirusScan	McAfee	0500 345 880

Communications

Procomm Plus	Datastorm	0800 789955
LapLink for Windows 95	Traveling Software	(01753) 818282

Computer Aided Design (CAD)

Visio Technical	Sharpware	(01372) 227900
Ashlar Vellum	Vellum Software	(01223) 300943
Sculptura	Aztec CAD	(0171) 9876543
Paracad +	CADlogic	(01223) 300943
Caddie	Vector Graphics	(01727) 830551
Autocad	Autodesk	(01483) 303322
Powerdraft	Bently Systems	(01344) 412233
Microstation 95	Bently Systems	(01344) 412233
Radan	Radan	(01225) 320320
Pro/Engineer	Definitive App	(01635) 874224
FloorPlan	FastTrack	(01923) 228796
Xcad	Xcad	(0181) 893 4000

Cookery

Mrs Beeton	One Shop Direct	(0181) 947 1001
Micro Kitchen Companion	One Shop Direct	(0181) 947 1001
Escoffier	Interactive Ideas	(0181) 447 9288
Healthy Indulgences	Softkey International	(0181) 789 2000
Cooking with Dom DeLuise	Comput-Ed	(01626) 889955
Schwartz World Cuisine	GSP	(01480) 496666

Databases

Visual FoxPro 3	Microsoft	(01734) 270001
Visual dBase	Borland Int	(01734) 320022
Database 2	IBM	(01705) 498151
Paradox	Borland	(0990) 561281

Desktop publishing

Pagemaker	Adobe	(0131) 451 6888
PagePlus	Serif	0800 92492
Publisher	Microsoft	0345 002000

QuarkXPress	Quark Systems	(01483) 454397
Corel Ventura	Channel Market	(01703) 814142
FrameMaker	Frame Technology	(0181) 6064100
Calamus 95	Jakes Graphic Des.	(0114) 2483420

Document image processing

File Magic Plus	Document Tech.	(0161) 763 4331
FilePower	Optika	(01483) 726222
Keyfile Enterprise	Dialog Image	(01442) 213222
PaperClip for Windows Network	Digital Doc. Systems	(0171) 431 1222

Drawing and graphics

| Smartsketch 95 | CGS Computer Supp | (0181) 679 7307 |
| CorelDRAW | Corel | 0800 581028 |

Home and garden design

FloorPlan Plus	FastCAD Europe	(01923) 246427
Europress 3D Garden Designer	Watford Electronics	(01582) 745555
Europress 3D Landscape Design	Watford Electronics	(01582) 745555
3D Landscape	FastTrak Software	(01923) 228796
Softkey Home Gardener	Watford Electronics	(01582) 745555

Integrated software suites

Office 97	Microsoft	0800 959595
Lotus SmartSuite	MrPC	(01282) 777888
PerfectOffice	Technomatic	(0181) 205 9558

Internet

Internet Chameleon	Leaf Distribution	(01256) 79777
MSK Internet Anywhere	System Science	(0171) 833 1022
Emmissary	Wollongong Value	(01344) 304242
UK Online	UK Online	(01749) 333333
Pipex Dial	Unipalm Pipex	0500 474739
NetLauncher	CompuServe	0800 289378
InternetSuite	Quarterdeck	(01245) 491190
InterAp	County Internet Sev	(01245) 348000

Labels

| Prism for Windows | MAP80 Systems | (01734) 731800 |

Learning and training

Learn Windows 95	DiscoverWare	0800 413078
Interactive Tutorials on CD	BVS	(01874) 611633

Management

Visual Staff Scheduler	LTS	(01386) 792617
Time Line Lite	Deepak Sareen	(0181) 423 8855
Super Office 3	Super Office	(01442) 871119
Tracker	Tracker Software	(01628) 488866
Project 95	Microsoft	0345 002000

MPEG players

Xing	Graphics Direct	(01635) 873000

Multilingual wordprocessors

Universal Word	Prestige Network	(01344) 303800
Accent	Accent Software	(01923) 208435
Linguawrite for Windows	Multi-Lingua	(0181) 974 6851
Wordmate	Prestige Network	(01344) 303880
Languagelink Pro for Windows	Language Link	(0181) 299 0067
UniType	Lingua	(01484) 689494

Multimedia authoring tools

Multimedia MasterClass	Independent Software	(01372) 745226
Macromedia Director	Macromedia	(01344) 761111
IconAuthor	Aimtech	(0171) 702 1575

Music and sound

Sound Studio Professional	Evolution Elect	(01525) 372621
Capella	Software Partners	(01926) 842998
Cubase	Tech-Mate	(01206) 793355
Finale	Millennium	(0115) 955 2200

Online dictionaries

Recognita Plus	SZKI	(00361) 2018925
Collins Inline	Harper-Collins	(01903) 873555

Optical character recognition

Textbridge	Xerox	(01734) 668421
OmniPage Pro	Caere UK	(0171) 630 5586

Programming languages

Visual C++	Microsoft	0345 002000
Visual BASIC	Microsoft	0345 002000
C and C++	Boland	0990 561281

Route planning

Route 66	Geographics Info	(0031) 318 554724
AutoRoute	Express Microsoft	0345 002000

Statistics

Unistat	Adept Scientific	(01462) 480055

Translation

Language Assistant	Globlink	0800 752 752
Power Translation	Globlink	0800 752 752

Utilities

First Aid 95	Roderick Manhattan	(0181) 875 4444
WINProbe	Quarterdeck	(01245) 496699
Sidekick 95	Starfish Software	(01675) 466467
Microsoft Plus	Microsoft	0345 002000
CleanSweep95	Quarterdeck	(01245) 496699
Norton Utilities	Symantec	0800 526495

Voice recognition

Kurzweil Voice	Responsive Systems	(0171) 602 4107

Word Processors

WordPro	Lotus	0800 123 222
Word for Windows 95	Microsoft	0345 002000
WordPerfect	Novell	(01344) 724100
WordStar	SoftKey	(0181) 789 2000

Appendix B
Magazines on PCs

There are numerous PC magazines on the market of varying quality. Although most come with a CD-ROM attached you will find that the material on it is of little value. Fortunately the editorial content is usually much better. All the magazines carry out reviews on hardware and software products and some are quite thorough and the opinions are worth due consideration.

Magazine Title	Publisher	Special features
PC Pro	Dennis Publication	CD-ROM
Personal Computer Magazine	VNU Business Publication	Limited circulation
PC Direct	Ziff-Davis Publication	Low cost yearly subscription and CD-ROM
PC Plus	Future Publishers	CD-ROM
PC User	emap Business Communications	Limited circulation
PC Magazine	Ziff-Davis Publication	Low-cost yearly subscription and CD-ROM
PC Advisor	IT Publishing	CD-ROM
Personal Computer World	VNU Business Publication	CD-ROM

Glossary

486. Microprocessor, made by Intel, found in PCs at the lower end of the market. Now available in three models: 486DX (33 MHz), 486DX2 (66 MHz) and the 486DX4 (100 MHz).

Asynchronous. A term used when describing data transfer between devices which may be operating at different speeds. It's necessary for the devices to have a hand-shake arrangement to enable exchange of data. Generally much slower than synchronous data flow.

Authoring software. Software specifically designed to enable multimedia presentations for a PC to be constructed easily and efficiently. It requires no formal computer programming experience and the design techniques can be mastered in a relatively short time (Chapter 4).

BIOS, Basic Input Output System. Software permanently resident in the PC that handles all the data flow to and from the PC's microprocessor to everything else in the PC (Chapter 2).

Boot-sector. A special area on the hard-disc (or floppy disc) which holds the start-up software which is loaded into the PC's RAM when the PC is powered up (Chapter 2).

Cache memory. During the operation of a program, data is loaded from the hard-disc and stored in the PC's RAM. When the CPU needs the data it is fetched from RAM. To speed up this process, when the data is fetched from RAM a copy of it is stored in cache memory which can be accessed much quicker than RAM. The next time the CPU wants the same data it is fetched from cache instead of RAM. This has the effect of speeding up the program execution (Chapter 2).

CD-ROM drive. An essential component of a modern PC able to read the data stored on CD-ROMs. Data are stored on CD-ROMs in the same way as on floppy-discs except the CD-ROM can hold over 600 MByte compared with 1.44 for a floppy disc. Normally multimedia data (video footage, images, sound files and audio files) are held on CD-ROMs (Chapters 2 and 3).

Central Processing Unit, CPU. The name frequently given to the microprocessor that acts as the central intelligence of a PC – see Pentium processor.

Chipset. Integrated circuits (ICs) that service the operational needs of the CPU in the PC. Normally come as a family and are designed specifically to match the needs of the CPU (Chapter 2).

CMOS RAM. A small amount of memory inside the PC that remains permanently on and is powered by a battery. It takes very little power and contains information relating to the configuration of the PC which is required by the CPU as the PC is switched on. The contents of the CMOS RAM can be changed by the user during the power-up phase. For example, if a new hard-disc is added to the PC the CMOS RAM will have to be modified so that the CPU will know of the existence of the new disc drive (Chapter 2).

Database. Commonly used for storing records of information on a PC. It allows the information to be stored in an ordered manner that allows easy cross-referencing and searching of common themes. An example product is Microsoft Access (Chapter 4).

Expansion bus. A feature on the motherboard of all PCs for expanding its functionality. It comprises a row of parallel connectors that are able to accommodate expansion cards. In current PCs you will find a mixture of ISA and PCI connectors (Chapter 2).

Expansion card. A card made up of electronic components that can be inserted into the expansion bus in the PC main unit. Expansion cards have the effect of extending the PC's functionality. For example, if you wished to add a fax facility to your PC, you could insert a fax expansion card to the PC (Chapter 2).

Floppy disc. Every PC is fitted with a floppy disc-drive which reads floppy discs. Floppy discs are flexible circular discs, covered with magnetic material and held within a 3¼ inch plastic case. They have a storage capacity of 1.44 Mbyte and can be used to store data for back-up purposes (Chapter 2).

Graphics. The collective term referring to the appearance of the information on the PC's screen (monitor). There are various graphics formats which affect the number of colours, the resolution and the speed of the screen refresh which is important for watching video material (Chapters 2 and 3).

Hard-disc. The main data storage unit in the PC. Unlike the floppy disc, the hard-disc comprises a stack of rigid platters coated with magnetic material. Storage capacities range from 200 Mbyte to several Gbyte depending on the design (Chapter 2). These days hard-discs are very reliable. However, they should always be backed up.

Hub. A device used in connecting several PCs together to form a network. The hub is an array of bridging circuits that allows any one PC to exchange information with other PCs on the network (Chapter 7).

Hypertext. A peculiar feature of computer stored information. A page of hypertext text will have certain words highlighted. As you mouse click on these you are led off to further information relating to the highlighted word. Encyclopaedias commonly use hypertext formats.

Icon. A feature on the PC's screen that when activated with a mouse point and click action leads the user to a new activity.

Integrated office suite. It has been recognised by software producers that commercial offices have many common PC requirements. These requirements have been distilled into a suite of software products known as an integrated office suite. A typical suite would contain a wordprocessor, a diary, a spreadsheet and a database (Chapter 4).

Internet. Also known as the Information Superhighway, it's an international network of computers offering accessible databases and personal information exchange. To access the Internet you require a service provider (Chapter 6).

ISA bus. A feature of the PC to allow its functionality to be expanded. Physically it is a row of slots on the PC's motherboard into which expansion cards are inserted; for example, a fax card. ISA (Industry Standard Architecture) was the first interface design. Today it is complemented by the PCI bus (Chapter 2).

Lap-top. A design of PC which is very compact and is usually the size of an A4 sheet of paper. Very convenient for people on the move. They are usually battery-powered and carry an extra price premium (Chapter 1).

Local Area Network. When several PCs are used in an office environment it's advantageous to allow them to talk to each other. This is achieved by networking them into a LAN (Local Area Network). A user on any one PC can access the facilities on any of the others on the LAN (Chapter 7).

Menu bar. All programs running under Microsoft Windows have a menu bar at the top of the screen. When the mouse is clicked on a menu item, a drop-down menu is produced to give further choices or required activities.

MIDI, Musical Instrument Digital Interface. A standard to allow electronics instruments to communicate with each other and with computers. All modern sound cards have an on-board MIDI connector to enable a PC to be linked up to a synthesiser (Chapter 3).

MMX Processor. Also known as the P55C, the MMX is a variant of the Pentium and has been designed to optimise multimedia processes; this is especially true for high intensive graphics applications such as games. Although software designed for the Pentium will run on MMX-based PCs, to capitalise on the MMX processor, software must be specifically compiled to run on it. On the whole it appears that the MMX does perform better than the Pentium even on software not specifically written for the MMX. Clock speeds for the MMX start at 166 MHz upwards beyond 200 MHz.

Modem. A device that allows your PC to communicate with other computers using the public telephone system. All modems have a telephone connector to allow them to be plugged into a telephone socket (Chapter 5).

Monitor. The screen on the PC that provides the visual information for the user. Colour monitors are normally available in four sizes, 14, 15, 17 and 21 inch. The images on the monitor are created by the graphics card that is situated in the main PC unit (Chapter 2).

Motherboard. A printed circuit board on which are situated the majority of electronics in the PC unit. The motherboard hosts the central processing unit, the expansion bus, the RAM, the chipset and cache memory (Chapter 2).

Mouse. An external hand-controlled unit with two or three buttons for controlling the position of the cursor (a pointer) on the screen. Software usually requires a **point and click** action which is performed by the user's movement of the mouse (Chapter 2).

Multimedia PC. A PC equipped with a sound card and CD-ROM drive that is able to run multimedia software such as video, sound and animation.

Operating system. A software environment under which a user can run programs. A modern operating system, such as Windows, allows several programs to run at the same time and enables data to be transferred from one program to another (Chapter 4).

Optical character recognition. A software product that is capable of converting an image of written text into a document file that can be used and edited by a wordprocessor (Chapter 4).

Parallel port. Usually required for connecting a printer to your PC.

PC card. To extend the functionality of a lap-top PC, many have an interface to house a PC card (also known as PCMCIA). Owing to the limited space available in a lap-top PC, the majority of peripherals are connected through the PC card socket.

PCI bus. To enhance the functionality of a PC it's possible to use an expansion card which is inserted to the expansion bus housed on the motherboard in the main PC's unit. On modern PCs the design of the bus conforms to the PCI standard which allows 32-bit data transfer (Chapter 2).

Pentium processor. A high performance microprocessor (central processing unit – CPU) manufactured by Intel. It's the successor to the 486 and is available in a number of clock speeds ranging from 75 MHz to 200 MHz (Chapter 2). It is found in the PC in a zero insertion force (ZIF) socket on the motherboard usually with a little fan or heat sink attached to it.

RAM. Before a program can be run by the CPU a copy of it is loaded into the PC's Random Access Memory (RAM) which is situated on the motherboard. RAM will also hold data used by the program and in general the more RAM you have the faster your programs will run. RAM is normally packaged in SIMMs (Chapter 2).

Scanner. A convenient device for converting a photograph of a page of text into a digital format that can be stored in the PC's memory. A scanner is normally used in combination with **optical character recognition** (OCR) software.

SCSI, Small Computer System Interface. A means of performing very rapid data transfer between peripherals and the PC (Chapter 2).

Serial port. Every PC has at least two serial ports. It is common practice to have the mouse connected to one and usually an external modem to the other. Sometimes you may even have a printer connected to a serial port especially if the printer is situated many metres away from the printer (Chapter 5).

SIMMs, Single Inline Memory Modules. The normal packages for RAM, usually 30 or 72 pin. There is an area on the motherboard which accommodates SIMMs directly. SIMMs today come in either 8, 16, 32 (or even larger) Mbyte blocks (Chapter 2).

Sound card. An expansion card, accommodated in the PC's expansion bus, for generating musical sounds and quality sound effects. Since it has its own audio amplifier it can be connected directly to stereo loudspeakers or alternatively to a hi-fi unit to produce the best results (Chapter 3).

Spreadsheet. A software product for handling large quantities of numbers that need to be manipulated and processed. A spreadsheet is designed as an array of cells which can be accessed individually and processed collectively (Chapter 4).

Synchronous. A term used when describing the data transfer between devices which are operating at the same speed. Usually data is configured into blocks or packets and transferred in bursts. Generally faster than asynchronous data flow.

Tower system. A design of PC unit that has greater height than width. Convenient when space is at a premium, a tower system can be stored under a desk leaving more space on the desk surface (Chapter 1).

Visual software. A range of software products that allows the programmer to construct graphical features easily on the screen. Used for creating tables, graphs and control icons with a visual language. Examples are Visual BASIC and Delphi (Chapter 4).

VL-bus. A design of expansion bus that was the predecessor to the PCI bus. You would probably find a VL-bus in a 486-based PC. It has now been largely superseded by the PCI bus (Chapter 2).

Windows for WorkGroups. The predecessor to Windows 95 was Windows 3.11 also known as Windows for WorkGroups because it contained software for allowing a number of PCs to be networked to form a workgroup – easy data exchange between each PC.

Windows. Windows is an advanced software operating system from Microsoft designed specifically for PCs. It allows several programs to be up and running at the same time and facilitates an exchange of information (data) between the active programs (Chapter 4).

Wordprocessor. Probably the most widely used software facility. A very convenient means of generating and manipulating text. By employing **cut and paste** techniques the user can move paragraphs and sentences around the document with absolute ease (Chapter 4).

Index

How To Books provide practical help on a large range of topics. They are available through all good bookshops or can be ordered direct from the distributors. Just tick the titles you want and complete the form on the following page.

___ Apply to an Industrial Tribunal (£7.99)
___ Applying for a Job (£8.99)
___ Applying for a United States Visa (£15.99)
___ Backpacking Round Europe (£8.99)
___ Be a Freelance Journalist (£8.99)
___ Be a Freelance Secretary (£8.99)
___ Become a Freelance Sales Agent (£9.99)
___ Becoming a Father (£8.99)
___ Buy & Run a Shop (£8.99)
___ Buy & Run a Small Hotel (£8.99)
___ Buying a Personal Computer (£9.99)
___ Career Networking (£8.99)
___ Career Planning for Women (£8.99)
___ Cash from your Computer (£9.99)
___ Choosing a Nursing Home (£9.99)
___ Choosing a Package Holiday (£8.99)
___ Claim State Benefits (£9.99)
___ Collecting a Debt (£9.99)
___ Communicate at Work (£7.99)
___ Conduct Staff Appraisals (£7.99)
___ Conducting Effective Interviews (£8.99)
___ Coping with Self Assessment (£9.99)
___ Copyright & Law for Writers (£8.99)
___ Counsel People at Work (£7.99)
___ Creating a Twist in the Tale (£8.99)
___ Creative Writing (£9.99)
___ Critical Thinking for Students (£8.99)
___ Dealing with a Death in the Family (£9.99)
___ Do Your Own Advertising (£8.99)
___ Do Your Own PR (£8.99)
___ Doing Business Abroad (£10.99)
___ Doing Business on the Internet (£12.99)
___ Doing Voluntary Work Abroad (£9.99)
___ Emigrate (£9.99)
___ Employ & Manage Staff (£8.99)
___ Find Temporary Work Abroad (£8.99)
___ Finding a Job in Canada (£9.99)
___ Finding a Job in Computers (£8.99)
___ Finding a Job in New Zealand (£9.99)
___ Finding a Job with a Future (£8.99)
___ Finding Work Overseas (£9.99)
___ Freelance DJ-ing (£8.99)
___ Freelance Teaching & Tutoring (£9.99)
___ Get a Job Abroad (£10.99)
___ Get a Job in Europe (£9.99)
___ Get a Job in France (£9.99)
___ Get a Job in Travel & Tourism (£8.99)
___ Get into Radio (£8.99)
___ Getting a Job in America (£10.99)
___ Getting a Job in Australia (£9.99)
___ Getting into Films & Television (£10.99)
___ Getting That Job (£8.99)
___ Getting your First Job (£8.99)
___ Going to University (£8.99)
___ Having a Baby (£8.99)

___ Helping your Child to Read (£8.99)
___ How to Study & Learn (£8.99)
___ Investing in People (£9.99)
___ Investing in Stocks & Shares (£9.99)
___ Keep Business Accounts (£7.99)
___ Know Your Rights at Work (£8.99)
___ Learning to Counsel (£9.99)
___ Live & Work in Germany (£9.99)
___ Live & Work in Greece (£9.99)
___ Live & Work in Italy (£8.99)
___ Live & Work in Portugal (£9.99)
___ Live & Work in the Gulf (£9.99)
___ Living & Working in America (£12.99)
___ Living & Working in Australia (£12.99)
___ Living & Working in Britain (£8.99)
___ Living & Working in China (£9.99)
___ Living & Working in Hong Kong (£10.99)
___ Living & Working in Israel (£10.99)
___ Living & Work in New Zealand (£9.99)
___ Living & Working in Saudi Arabia (£12.99)
___ Living & Working in the Netherlands (£9.99)
___ Living Away From Home (£8.99)
___ Making a Complaint (£8.99)
___ Making a Video (£9.99)
___ Making a Wedding Speech (£8.99)
___ Manage a Sales Team (£8.99)
___ Manage an Office (£8.99)
___ Manage Computers at Work (£8.99)
___ Manage People at Work (£8.99)
___ Manage Your Career (£8.99)
___ Managing Budgets & Cash Flows (£9.99)
___ Managing Credit (£8.99)
___ Managing Meetings (£8.99)
___ Managing Projects (£8.99)
___ Managing Your Personal Finances (£8.99)
___ Managing Yourself (£8.99)
___ Market Yourself (£8.99)
___ Mastering Book-Keeping (£8.99)
___ Mastering Business English (£8.99)
___ Master GCSE Accounts (£8.99)
___ Master Public Speaking (£8.99)
___ Migrating to Canada (£12.99)
___ Obtaining Visas & Work Permits (£9.99)
___ Organising Effective Training (£9.99)
___ Passing Exams Without Anxiety (£8.99)
___ Passing That Interview (£8.99)
___ Plan a Wedding (£8.99)
___ Planning Your Gap Year (£8.99)
___ Preparing a Business Plan (£8.99)
___ Publish a Book (£9.99)
___ Publish a Newsletter (£9.99)
___ Raise Funds & Sponsorship (£7.99)
___ Rent & Buy Property in France (£9.99)
___ Rent & Buy Property in Italy (£9.99)
___ Research Methods (£8.99)

How To Books

___ Retire Abroad (£8.99)
___ Return to Work (£7.99)
___ Run a Voluntary Group (£8.99)
___ Setting up Home in Florida (£9.99)
___ Setting Up Your Own Limited Company (£9.99)
___ Spending a Year Abroad (£8.99)
___ Start a Business from Home (£7.99)
___ Start a New Career (£6.99)
___ Starting to Manage (£8.99)
___ Starting to Write (£8.99)
___ Start Word Processing (£8.99)
___ Start Your Own Business (£8.99)
___ Study Abroad (£8.99)
___ Study & Live in Britain (£7.99)
___ Studying at University (£8.99)
___ Studying for a Degree (£8.99)
___ Successful Grandparenting (£8.99)
___ Successful Mail Order Marketing (£9.99)
___ Successful Single Parenting (£8.99)
___ Survive Divorce (£8.99)
___ Surviving Redundancy (£8.99)
___ Taking in Students (£8.99)
___ Taking on Staff (£8.99)
___ Taking Your A-Levels (£8.99)
___ Teach Abroad (£8.99)
___ Teach Adults (£8.99)
___ Teaching Someone to Drive (£8.99)
___ Travel Round the World (£8.99)
___ Understand Finance at Work (£8.99)
___ Use a Library (£7.99)
___ Using the Internet (£9.99)

___ Winning Consumer Competitions (£8.99)
___ Winning Presentations (£8.99)
___ Work from Home (£8.99)
___ Work in an Office (£7.99)
___ Work in Retail (£8.99)
___ Work with Dogs (£8.99)
___ Working Abroad (£14.99)
___ Working as a Holiday Rep (£9.99)
___ Working as an Au Pair (£8.99)
___ Working in Japan (£10.99)
___ Working in Photography (£8.99)
___ Working in the Gulf (£10.99)
___ Working in Hotels & Catering (£9.99)
___ Working on Contract Worldwide (£9.99)
___ Working on Cruise Ships (£9.99)
___ Write a Press Release (£9.99)
___ Write & Sell Computer Software (£9.99)
___ Write for Television (£8.99)
___ Writing a CV that Works (£8.99)
___ Writing a Non Fiction Book (£9.99)
___ Writing a Report (£8.99)
___ Writing a Textbook (£12.99)
___ Writing an Assignment (£8.99)
___ Writing an Essay (£8.99)
___ Writing & Publishing Poetry (£9.99)
___ Writing & Selling a Novel (£8.99)
___ Writing Business Letters (£8.99)
___ Writing for Publication (£8.99)
___ Writing Reviews (£9.99)
___ Writing Romantic Fiction (£9.99)
___ Writing Science Fiction (£9.99)
___ Writing Your Dissertation (£8.99)

To: Plymbridge Distributors Ltd, Plymbridge House, Estover Road, Plymouth PL6 7PZ. Customer Services Tel: (01752) 202301. Fax: (01752) 202331.

Please send me copies of the titles I have indicated. Please add postage & packing (UK £1, Europe including Eire, £2, World £3 airmail).

☐ I enclose cheque/PO payable to Plymbridge Distributors Ltd for £ [   ]

☐ Please charge to my ☐ MasterCard, ☐ Visa, ☐ AMEX card.

Account No. [   ]

Card Expiry Date [ ] 19 [ ] ☎ Credit Card orders may be faxed or phoned.

Customer Name (CAPITALS) ....

Address ....

.... Postcode...............

Telephone............................. Signature ....

Every effort will be made to despatch your copy as soon as possible but to avoid possible disappointment please allow up to 21 days for despatch time (42 days if overseas). Prices and availability are subject to change without notice.

Code BPA